UNBRIDLED SUCCESS

How the secret lives of horses can impact your *leadership*, *teamwork* and *communication* skills

UNBRIDLED
SUCCESS

How the secret lives of horses
can impact your *leadership*,
teamwork and *communication* skills

JULIA FELT🐎N

ecademyPRESS
www.ecademy-press.com

UNBRIDLED SUCCESS

How the secret lives of horses can impact your *leadership*, *teamwork* and *communication* skills

First published in 2012 by Ecademy Press

48 St Vincent Drive, St Albans, Herts, AL1 5SJ UK

info@ecademy-press.com

www.ecademy-press.com

Available online and from all good bookstores

Cover design by Michael Inns
Artwork by Karen Gladwell

Printed on acid-free paper from managed forests.
This book is printed on demand, so no copies will
be remaindered or pulped.

ISBN 978-1-908746-51-1

Contents

Acknowledgements

There are so many people that have touched me during my life's journey that I am indebted to, as they have helped shape who I am today. To my parents for their enduring support and guidance and for introducing me to horses during my childhood, and then at least for a few years, allowing me to live the dream of a pony-mad youngster.

To my business mentors John Assaraf, Roger Hamilton, Frank Croston, Marvin Rust and Alex Kyriakidis. Thank you for your guidance and support. And to all the people I have ever had the opportunity to work with, especially the HotelBenchmark™ team; I appreciate your contribution to my life and for creating such great experiences that I have been able to learn from.

To my first equine mentor, the late Kellie Gibbs of the Epona Horse Rescue in Colorado who gave me the space to explore how to build a relationship with a horse based on mutual trust and respect. Thank you for believing in me when I didn't believe that I could do it. I miss your generosity of spirit and love and commitment to helping horses.

Carolyn Resnick, my equine mentor and great friend, opened my eyes to the transformational power of horses. My internship with Carolyn was a pivotal point in my life as I began to realise the amazing life lessons that horses could teach me. Thank you Carolyn and I am honoured and privileged to be able to share your work with the world.

Dave and Sharon Harris of Acorn 2 Oaks for their unrelenting support in helping me attain my Licensed HorseDream Partner status, so that I could combine my corporate experience with my equine passion and translate that into a viable business venture. You are both an inspiration to me.

To Mindy Gibbins -Klein who encouraged and mentored me to write this book and her fabulous team at Ecademy Press, thank you. Without your input this manuscript would still be in my head, or best on my desk. And to all my other friends and colleagues who have helped me along the way – you know who you are – thank you.

I would like to acknowledge all the horses that have been part of my life – whether for a few fleeting hours or over a decade. Each of you has shared your wisdom with me and touched my heart. For the lessons you all shared with me, whether I learned them at the time or not until some years later, thank you. You have all shaped my life to help me become the best that I can be.

Finally, special thanks goes to my amazing herd of horses – Toby, Charlie, Bracken, Thistle, Red and Bunny – the best teachers in the world. You continue to challenge me and let me be your student. For that I am so grateful. I just hope that I do you all proud and allow others to experience the magical lessons that you continue to teach me

Introduction

"A Horse Whisperer is a master of non-verbal communication, and it is by working with horses that we can interpret and develop an individual's relationship and communication skills."

They say *'Horses are the greatest teachers'* and I could not agree more. Over the years, horses have taught me some of the best life and business lessons I could ever have learned. Admittedly, I did not always understand some of these lessons at the time, but now upon reflection I can see how horses have been masters at teaching me key business and life skills including:

- *How to be a leader that others will follow*
- *How to build trust*
- *How to communicate effectively*
- *How to manage team members*
- *How to perceive oneself and how to be perceived by others*
- *How to be authentic and congruent*
- *How to achieve goals with integrity*

It is my sincere hope that in this book I can reveal to you how horses can be such great teachers, so that you too can experience their magical power and benefit from their insights.

I was eight years old when my mum took me and my brother for our first riding lesson at Highfield Stables. I rode an old bay pony called Quickie and my brother rode a pony called Cindy. I remember that day so clearly, as if it was yesterday. Never, though, in my wildest dreams did I realise that I had just met the best teachers there are, who would impact my life so profoundly over the coming years, typically showing up at just the right time to help steer me on my journey.

I never owned my own pony whilst I was growing up but instead spent every weekend and school holiday helping at the local riding school. I was meant to get a free ride as payment for my work but that rarely happened. My dad got very angry as he felt that I was being exploited but I didn't care; it was never about the riding for me (although I do love to ride) but rather my happiness came from just being with the horses. They provided me with a sense of belonging that I rarely experienced anywhere else. I always felt at home with the horses, they were my best friends and I shared all my secrets with them.

As pony-mad as I was and despite my best attempts at trying to get a pony, it never happened. In the summer of 1977 I thought I had persuaded my dad to allow me to share a bay pony called Fudge, but my dreams were dashed when I was sent off to boarding school instead. I remember crying when I was left at school because I missed all the horses at Highfield Stables.

During my early teenage years horses took a back seat in my life, but I was still convinced that I wanted to carve out a career working with them. However, I was persuaded that I needed to 'get a proper job' and so my corporate career began. On reflection, this was the first time I was aware of giving away my personal power and allowing someone else to influence my life. I went with the flow and did not make a stand for what I wanted so much. I trusted someone else's judgment more than my own, and I never listened to my intuition.

I was successful in my corporate career working for companies like Andersen and Deloitte, as well as a few famous hotel companies along the way, but I always yearned to be with horses and never knew how I could combine my two passions; I always felt it was one or the other. Then on a windy, rainy November evening in 2003, my friend Beverley dragged me along to a Monty Roberts demonstration at Towerlands Equestrian Centre in Essex. I was mesmerised by the way he could connect with horses and so I began to study his work. By this time, my city salary had allowed me to purchase my first horse, Toby. In fact, interestingly he showed up at a pivotal time in my career. Andersen was going through the fallout of the Enron fiasco and there were very real fears that we might all lose our jobs. To this day I am still bemused that one of the top five largest accountancy firms in the world could implode so quickly. I think everyone was astonished by this, but for me it helped me gain real perspective on my life. What did I want and why? It was apparent that I could not rely on my employer for the comfort and security they had once offered. I needed to become responsible for myself and my destiny.

At this time I also read Monty Roberts' book *Horse Sense for People* in which he shares how his principles of trust and non-violence can be applied to both the home and the workplace. As I read the book I began to draw parallels of how my behaviour at work was impacting my team members. It was very insightful. I began to apply what I was reading and achieved some remarkable results. I became a student of the horse and over the next decade studied all I could about horse psychology and people psychology to help me align the two modalities. A chance encounter with Paul Hunting, the pioneer of Horse Accelerated Transformation™ in the UK, revealed a way for me to combine all my learning and so another door was opened.

Paul introduced me to the work of internationally renowned horse trainer Carolyn Resnick, and when I agreed to become her apprentice to help her write her next book I never knew what a profound impact being her student would have. Carolyn has an innate ability to understand and interpret horse behaviour in a way that I had never encountered before. Her work is entirely based on how to build a partnership with a horse, based on companionship, trust and mutual respect. What she taught me, however, went way beyond horse training as she shared with me the lessons that horses had taught her over the years. The more time I spent with her the more I became consciously aware of the great lessons that horses had taught me in my own life. It was just that at the time I had been blind to those lessons. Upon returning to the UK, after having spent six months in the USA with Carolyn Resnick, I gained my Horse Assisted Coaching qualifications and became a Licensed HorseDream Partner. Finally I was able to fully integrate everything I had experienced and reflect on what I had learned. If I had only known then what I know now, how even more successful and easier my corporate career could have been.

Today I describe myself as *The Business Horse Whisperer* and I am passionate about helping companies realise the great untapped potential that horses can offer them in teaching their team members about themselves in an honest and authentic way. As team members become more aware of their influence and impact on others, self-esteem and engagement improve, the net result being greater success for the business.

My desire is that this book informs and educates you to the benefits that Horse Assisted Coaching could offer you on both a personal and business level. If you feel any resistance to reading this book then you might want to examine why and where else this behaviour is showing up in your life. And if after reading this book you decide that Horse Assisted Coaching is not for you or your company, then great – but at least you have had some insight into the amazing transformational benefits that can result from interacting with horses. As the Buddhist proverb goes: *'When the student is ready the teacher will appear.'* Your teacher may not be a horse but my sincere hope is that some day it might be.

A New Coaching Paradigm Unbridled

'There is something about the outside of a horse that is good for the inside of a man.'

Sir Winston Churchill

A New Coaching
Paradigm Unbridled

'There is something about the outside of a horse that is good for the inside of a man.'

Sir Winston Churchill

The immortal words of the late, great Sir Winston Churchill are as apt today as they were some 100 years ago when he spoke them. So what is it about a horse that is good for the *'inside of a man?* Well, as Sir Winston Churchill recognised, horses can teach us a whole number of lessons that can help us in life, whether in the barn or the boardroom. Some life skills that horses can teach us include leadership, communication, teamwork, relationship-building, authenticity, congruency and how to build trust and respect with others.

Over the last three years the world has experienced a paradigm shift. The current social and economic climate is providing us with some of the most challenging times ever – both on a professional and personal level. Within business a spate of downsizing and cost-cutting measures means that we have team members in roles that some are ill-equipped to fulfil. Team dynamics have changed and yet we expect our people to deliver even more. For individuals this can cause stress and anxiety.

Innovative, forward-thinking companies have realised that traditional training and coaching methods are no longer cost-effective in helping develop systemic change in their team members, so a new approach to coaching, learning, training and development is required – one that engages the team members, challenges and helps them reflect on their skills and attributes. Horse Assisted Coaching is a new field of action-based learning in which individuals develop their own style of leadership through a variety of interactive exercises with horses. Absolutely no horsemanship skills are required to engage in a Horse Assisted Coaching session and all the work is conducted on the ground – there is no need to ride – which is why this coaching appeals to all types of people and their organisations.

So if you are wondering what Horse Assisted Coaching is and how importantly it could benefit you, your team members and/or company, then read on as I will be sharing with you the answers to all these questions and many more.

What is Experiential Learning?

> *'Experience is not what happens to you,*
> *it is what you do with what happens to you.'*
> **Aldous Huxley**

Action-based or experiential learning essentially means that learning and development is achieved through personally determined experience and involvement rather than on received teaching or training, typically in a group, by observation, listening, study of theory or hypothesis, or some transfer of skills or knowledge. The expression 'hands-on' is commonly used to describe this type of learning and teaching and an apprenticeship is a great example of where on-the-job, hands-on training is used to teach new manual skills such as carpentry, car mechanics etc.

Tim Buividas of the Corporate Learning Institute (CLI) defines experiential learning as:

> *"Activities that include any active learning experience which offers a chance to learn from failure, success and everything in between. It has to include the possibility of transferring learning back to the workplace. Examples of active learning or experiential learning activities include ropes courses, problem-solving games, and many indoor events. Any indoor active learning session includes a learning cycle. For an experiential session to be effective, participants have to experience, review, discuss, and apply their experiences."*

The earliest beginnings of experiential learning are rooted in programmes like Project Adventure and Outward Bound. Corporations around the world adopted outdoor experiential learning as evidenced by a famous segment in the 1990s sitcom *Murphy Brown.* Its use began to diminish as other popular concepts replaced it, from the emotional intelligence movement to strengths-based leadership. But like the timeless need that corporations have for personal commitment, team collaboration and innovative risk-taking, experiential learning continues to thrive.

A somewhat overlooked but what I believe is a very important facet of experiential learning is that it involves growing a person from the inside out, whereas conventional teaching and training is the transfer of capability into the person from the outside. Experiential learning is adaptable for individual styles, preferences, strength and direction and, as such, it is more likely to produce positive emotional effects than conventionally prescribed training – notably confidence, self-esteem and a sense of personal value and purpose.

The primary driver of experiential learning is to help the individual grow, learn and develop their own direction, whereas in conventional teaching and training the needs of the business are the primary driver of the learning content, design, delivery and assessment. Until recently, the notion of developing people as individuals was regarded by many employers as less efficient and effective than conventional training and teaching. Yet the paradigm shift that has happened, combined with the advances in technology, particularly social media, is changing all this. In our 'networked economy' partnerships – strategic and tactical, customer and supplier, personal and organisational – are essential to competitive effectiveness. As a result, leadership is no longer defined by what a leader does but rather as a process that engenders and is a result of relationships. The ability to influence and get results is determined by how the leader shows up – a concept that we will examine later in the book – hence the requirement for development programmes that grow the individual and help them develop themselves from the inside out.

The difference between experiential learning and conventional training and teaching can be summarised as follows:

Conventional Training	Experiential Learning
Theoretical – training centred/focused	*Doing it – learning-centred/focused*
Prescribed, fixed design and content	*Flexible, open possibilities*
For external needs (organisation, exams)	*For internal growth and discovery*
Transfers, explains knowledge and skills	*Develops knowledge, skills, emotions via experience*
Fixed structure delivery/ facilitation	*Unstructured, not delivered, minimal facilitation*
Time-bound, measurable components (mainly)	*Not time-bound, more difficult to measure*

Horse Assisted Coaching is fundamentally based around learning by doing, which is the way humans learn best as it engages all the senses. It accesses your ability to learn concepts through three channels:

- *Kinaesthetic learning through physical activity*

- *Metaphorical learning through symbolism and comparative conceptual application*

- *Metaphysical learning through core energy connections*

In other words, it accesses your body, mind and spirit to internalise what you learn. Research in 1999 by Smolowe, Butler and Murray estimates that we remember only 20% of what we hear and 50% of what we see but retain fully 80% of what we do. This is why activity-based or action learning experiences have greater sticking power and result in more systemic change in individuals than traditional style training where students sit and receive information in a lecture- style format.

The famous Chinese philosopher Confucius said in c450 BC:

'I hear, and I forget. I see and I remember,
I do and I understand.'

In my own life I always opt to learn from experience rather than just listening and watching. In fact I remember when I was at university studying Hotel Management and we had to learn basic culinary skills. I was great on the theory but put me into a kitchen and disaster loomed. On one particular occasion I remember I was asked to make a Victoria sponge cake – not too tricky you would think, but I managed to get the proportion of ingredients wrong, resulting in a cake that barely rose. Then, to add insult to injury, when I went to decorate the cake with cream and jam to disguise the flat, now somewhat burnt cake, I put jam on two-thirds of the cake base. Then, for some reason I will never comprehend, I realised that I had put too much jam on and cut the cake base into two-thirds leaving just one-third for the top. To this day I still don't know why I couldn't figure out that I could cut the cake into halves and it would still work. However, rest assured

I have never forgotten that lesson. I'm sure you can think of similar situations where you were told something but it took actually doing the action for you to fully understand the process for creating the result.

The benefits of experiential learning can be further realised when one considers that latest anecdotal research estimates that today on average only 4% of what is learnt in the classroom is retained if changes are not implemented immediately upon return to the workplace. We live in an information society and the bombardment of information we have is just overwhelming. Our brains simply can't cope with the 2-4,000 bits of information that our conscious minds take in every second. Combine that with the 400 billion bits of data our unconscious mind experiences per second and it is not surprising that we have to generalise, distort and delete facts at an alarming speed that don't fit or align with what is on our current radar screen. This is the reason that more and more training and coaching programmes are adding an experiential element to their offering, and, whilst classroom-based experiential learning can be beneficial, the profound impact of off-site experiential learning in the countryside with horses magnifies the benefits, in my opinion, at least tenfold.

Different Types of Experiential Learning

There are a wide variety of experiential learning activities available on the market today that are physically and/ or psychologically demanding. All the activities work on the same premise that by removing someone from their comfort zone, they are able to grow and develop through experiencing another perspective on life. It is not about the activity *per se* but rather the lessons that the participants receive regarding their own strengths and weaknesses, and the insights they gain into their own internal resources. Faced with a challenging situation with which they are unfamiliar, participants often let down their mask, allowing their true authentic self to emerge. Through the repeated debriefing and probing about each learning experience, participants start to gain some real insight into how and why they behave in the way they do, and the consequences of those actions both for themselves and others. The activity becomes a metaphor for what is happening in a person's life and provides a mirror to reflect back information about their personality style, leadership style, communication ability and team-working skills.

Whilst on the surface it might appear that these courses are aimed at developing leadership and team-working skills, in fact their purpose is much greater as the experience often helps the participant explore their fears, build trust in themselves and others and develop their leadership skills in a supportive and non-threatening environment away from the workplace. These activities stretch people mentally, intellectually, emotionally and spiritually.

From my own perspective, I have always found that it is when I have been taken out my comfort zone to a place that I am not familiar with and asked to engage in activities with which I am often initially uncomfortable that I have experienced significant insight and learning. In my opinion, the results of any experiential learning activity are definitely worth more than the sum of its parts.

My own first experience of experiential learning in a corporate setting occurred in early 2000 when I attended an outward bound course. I was sent with one other team member and a group of other managers to deepest Cumbria where we spent a week isolated in a hotel in the middle of nowhere. Each day comprised a series of classroom and physical activities including high ropes (which given that I'm afraid of heights was terrifying), rock climbing and abseiling. There were also challenges that combined mental and physical tasks in a team such as building a raft and then getting the team to the other side of the lake. What I still recall to this today was the fact I surprised myself by how creative I could be with my ability to think out of the box to find solutions. Up to that point I would never have described myself as creative, and yet during that experience I discovered skills I had that I probably never would have uncovered in a classroom setting.

Furthermore I still remember sitting outside on the patio on the last day of the course with one of the tutors. We had been asked to review the week and set out our own personal and business goals for the next twelve months. During that time of reflection I had such a massive AHA! moment about my own situation that I remember breaking down in tears as I came to realise the impact my thinking and actions were having, both on myself and others. Let's just say that this revelation had a profound impact on my life, and following the course I made some significant changes in my life which ultimately resulted in me becoming a happier person and, as a consequence, a better leader for myself and my team.

How Experiential Learning Works

So how and why is experiential learning such a powerful experience for people? Well, its power lies in the fact that learning occurs at a limbic level in the brain rather in the neo-cortex level. To understand this better, let me share with you in simple terms how the brain operates. Our brain weighs approximately three pounds and it is the body's computer. It controls all the functions of the body, as well as our emotions and thoughts. In simple terms the brain is composed of three main areas:

- **The Reptilian Brain** – *this is the oldest of the three and controls the body's vital functions such as heart rate, breathing, body temperature and balance. It is our instinctive mind. The main structures found in the reptilian brain are the brainstem and the cerebellum.*

- **The Mammalian Brain** – *also known as the limbic system – records emotional experiences, those memories of behaviour that produce agreeable and disagreeable experiences. The main structures of the limbic system are the hippocampus, the amygdala and the hypothalamus. The limbic brain is where we make value judgments, either consciously or unconsciously, that exert such a strong influence on our behaviour.*

- **The Frontal Lobe** – *also known as the neo-cortex – this accounts for 35-40% of the human brain and has been described as the 'CEO of the brain'. It is the part of the brain that is responsible for focus, concentration, learning and the power of observation. It connects us to the quantum field of intelligence.*

The other factor to be aware of is that our brain is made up of two sides. Many of us have heard the expression of people being described as 'right' or 'left' brain. Left-brained people are generally very analytical, structured and organised – some might describe them as 'anally-retentive.' Other people are very right-brained, meaning that they are generally very arty, creative, rhythmic, think in pictures and are very imaginative. Most people generally have a default setting; however that is not to say that the other side of the brain cannot be developed and learn. In fact it is this ability that makes each and every one of us unique. However, what many people are not aware of is the fact that the brain is made up of the conscious and unconscious mind, and the relative importance of these. These differences are summarised in the table below.

CONSCIOUS MIND	UNCONSCIOUS MIND
17% of brain mass	*Power centre*
2-4% of actual perceptions and behaviours	*96-98% of all behaviour automatic*
Processes 2-4,000 bits of information per second	*Processes 400 billion bits of information per second*
Looks for patterns and images that are familiar, rejects those that aren't	*Controls our habitual responses*
Part of you that thinks and reasons	*Sees in pictures and patterns*
Short-term memory and can only process one to three events at a time	*Cannot tell real from imagined*

The unconscious mind is incredibly powerful as it controls 96-98% of our habits. As you are reading this book you do not have to think consciously to breathe, or get your heart to pump blood around your body. These functions are happening automatically. They occur on autopilot. However, it is not just our bodily functions that can operate on autopilot; many daily actions also happen without us being aware of them. Just think about it. How many of you consciously think about cleaning your teeth every morning and evening? I bet very few. It is just something that we do instinctively, it has become a habit. Likewise, if you drive the same route to work every day I'm sure you have experienced occasions when you have reached your destination and have no recollection of how you got there. Your unconscious just took over and got you there as if by magic. So how has this happened? It has happened because driving your car to work has become an unconscious competence.

The conscious competence model explains the process and stages of learning a new skill (or behaviour, ability, technique, etc.) as follows:

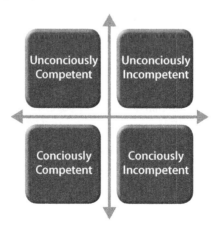

So when you first start learning an activity you are unconsciously incompetent as you don't know the activity, let alone how to undertake it. Let's take the example of learning to drive. Before you even start to learn to drive you are unconsciously incompetent as you have never driven before and so have no clue about how a car works and how to drive it. As you start driving lessons you become consciously incompetent as you realise what you don't know. You start to understand that you don't know when to change gears and when to signal. With more practice and experience you become consciously competent. You now know how to drive the car but it requires great effort as you continually have to think what to do next. Once you have advanced you become unconsciously competent and driving the car seems effortless. You do not need to think when to change gear for example, it just happens naturally. What has happened is that the activity of driving a car has been embedded in your unconscious and has become a habit as the neural pathways of learning have developed.

When we engage in experiential learning activities we help these neural pathways fire and so the learning becomes embedded in our limbic brain. The reason this is so profound is that scientific research has shown that more neural pathways travel from the limbic brain to the neo-cortex rather than the other way round. It is because learning happens on an unconscious level that the results of experiential learning can be profound and why these types of programmes provide a greater return on investment for companies compared to programmes that focus on verbal, classroom (neo-cortex) approaches. From my own experience – and the initial outward bound course in Cumbria is one such example – experiential learning has always delivered faster, deeper and, most importantly, a sustainable impact for me and my team members, both professionally and personally as, unlike cognitive learning, once we have learned to do these things and had these experiences we do not forget them.

The Experiential Learning Cycle

There has been much research conducted on the experiential learning cycle and perhaps the most notable research and documentation has been related to the David Kolb Learning Cycle. In essence, experiential learning comprises four activities:

- *Act – Do It*
- *Reflect On What Happened*
- *Review Why It Happened*
- *Apply The Learnings*

Martin Thompson of MTA, who is an expert in the field of experiential learning, states: '*The essence of effective experiential learning is that the entire process is centred on the learner – not the task, not the organisational objective, not the qualification standard, not the group and certainly not the trainer's or teacher's personal experience.*' In this respect the underpinning philosophy of well-executed experiential learning has much in common with good modern coaching and facilitated decision-making methodology, both of which place the learner at the centre of the issue.

The success, therefore, of any experiential approach to learning is that the learner needs to be motivated and engaged in the learning process. They need to want to act and then be prepared to reflect and review what happened before coming up with alternative strategies and plans of action that they could implement. Whilst experiential learning can occur without facilitation as it relies on the individual's capacity to learn, generally the most effective learning occurs when participants are asked probing questions by the facilitators. These often cause the individual to make a step change and gain real insight into what was happening by simply adding a new perspective on what transpired. One of the most important things to remember about experiential learning is that no one can predict what learning an individual will take from an activity. **Two people can undertake the same task and get completely different results, and this is the beauty of this type of learning. Each participant takes what they want and need from the experience.** Furthermore, the learning can occur on more than one level and it is not uncommon for participants to experience breakthroughs some time after the event when a seemingly innocuous activity triggers a memory recall and the participant suddenly gets the missing 'piece of the jigsaw puzzle'.

In the late 1990s, outward bound, high-rope courses and team-building events were often regarded as a 'jolly' – an excuse to get out of the office and have a good time. Unfortunately, in my experience this mindset still exists today which is why companies are prepared to invest thousands of pounds in putting their employees through classroom-based leadership training programmes instead of looking at creative experiential learning options. As someone who has participated in a myriad of different experiential learning days, I can honestly say that these training days have been some of the toughest and most insightful days I have ever had. When that 'light-bulb moment' occurs and you finally see how certain behaviour has been affecting you and others, and understand the consequences of continuing in this manner, then real, long-lasting change is possible. Some might argue that you could get these same insights in a classroom, and maybe that is true, but the real advantage of experiential learning is that you get a visceral experience, a whole body experience. The learnings get embedded deep within the limbic system and have emotional energy attached to them, which is why it is easier to implement these changes. Just think about it: we could all decide to go on a diet tomorrow and indeed many of us have tried dieting throughout our lives. So why is it that 97% of us fail to stay committed to our diets? The reason is that we revert to our subconscious patterns of behaviour and thought, our old habits. However, with limbic learning we start to rewire those old habits and embed new habits in their place. This for me is the fundamental reason why experiential learning is so profound.

Evolution of Horses Helping People

Horses have been helping people learn important life skills since time immemorial. At the beginning of this chapter we noted Sir Winston Churchill's profound statement about horses: *'There is something about the outside of a horse that is good for the inside of a man.'* Churchill was one of the greatest UK leaders we have ever seen, leading England through some of the most challenging conditions that this country has ever experienced. It is no surprise then that he was also an excellent horseman. Other examples of great leaders who were also great horsemen are former US presidents George Washington and Ronald Regan. In fact, if we think about it, in days gone by, before the advent of motorised vehicles, the horse was the mainstay of transportation for most people. The horse carried great leaders into battle and there are numerous stories about the great partnerships that existed between man and horse. Perhaps the best documented would be Alexander the Great and, in 2003, the Austrian management trainer and leadership lecturer Fritz Hendrich gave his book *Horse Sense* the subtitle: *How Alexander the Great first conquered a horse and then an empire. Three steps to the charisma of leadership.* However, it is only in recent years that we have begun to realise what many of these early pioneers knew: horses can be great teachers. We just need to listen and connect with them and we can learn more about ourselves than months of classroom learning can give us.

Although a relatively new modality in the corporate world, the concept of horses helping people has been around since the 1990s. Some of the early pioneers of this work include Barbara Rector and Arianna Strozzi in the USA who initially recognised the therapeutic benefits that horses could bring to people afflicted by either mental or physical disease. It was not until 1998 that a German former actor and IT trainer called Gerhard Krebs began offering experiential learning programmes to corporate clients. In 2004 he established the European Association of Horse Assisted Educators (EAHAE) and started training people to become Licensed HorseDream Partners, coaching people in how to deliver Horse Assisted Education to companies. Since then, a number of organisations have emerged offering a range of Horse Assisted Coaching Programmes. At one end of the continuum there are organisations like the Equine Assisted Growth and Learning Association (EGALA) who are focused on improving the mental health of individuals, families and groups through the work of Equine Psychotherapy, whilst at the other end of the spectrum is HorseDream, who focus predominantly on helping companies develop their team members in the key skills of leadership, communication and building trust.

Within the industry there are also organisations focused on helping children, women and even autistic children, as in the case of the *Horse Boy* programme. The *Horse Boy Method* was pioneered by Rupert Isaacson who noted that his severely autistic son's ability to communicate improved radically when he was in the presence of horses. This started a journey which led in 2007 to Rupert, his wife Kristin and Rowan, his autistic son, riding across Mongolia together – a journey that became the book and film *The Horse Boy*. Increasingly, Horse Assisted Coaching is being used to help army veterans cope with their reintegration into society after their war-torn experiences abroad, and scientific research has shown how horses can help people suffering with Post Traumatic Stress Disorder (PTSD).

So how come an industry that has such a diverse target audience can be the best kept secret there is? Part of the reason is that the industry is highly fragmented with most practitioners being solo entrepreneurs. There is a lack of co-ordination and co-operation within the sector and yet everyone involved in Horse Assisted Coaching agrees that there is something magical about the way horses can help people. Furthermore, the industry is referred to by a plethora of names, making sourcing a provider of these services more challenging. Other common names for the industry include: Equine Facilitated Learning, Horse Assisted Education, Horse Assisted Learning, Equine Assisted Coaching, Equine Guided Leadership Development, Equine Guided Education and Coaching, Equine Assisted Coaching, Equine Assisted Therapy and Equine Facilitated Personal Development.

Why Horses?

So what is it that enables horses to be such great teachers and healers of our souls? What is it about the outside of a horse that is good for the inside of a man and allows them to help us confront parts of our being that we would rather hide and gain the AHA! – or as I like to refer to them, Accelerated Horse Awareness™ – moments that can cause such profound changes in our lives?

The therapeutic effect that animals can have on people's lives has often been noted and it is one of the reasons why 27 million people in the UK are pet owners. Dogs and cats are the most popular pets, accounting for nearly 54% of the market. However, incredibly there are around 1.3 million horses owned by around 550,000 people.

It has often been noted that the mere presence of an animal can help people's stress levels. In the late 1990s, Karen Allen, a researcher at the State University of New York School of Medicine, conducted some research with a group of stressed, frantic stockbrokers. They were each given a dog to care for and their stress levels monitored over a period of months. What was interesting about the research was it demonstrated that when people were in the presence of the dogs (who by now had become trusted companions) they had a much lower stress level than people without dogs. Whilst initially Allen thought that the act of stroking the dog could be responsible for releasing endorphins that lowered stress levels, the surprising result was that stress levels fell simply by being in the presence of the animal. So what was happening? There was some connection occurring in the quantum field of emotional energy whereby the owners were able to be moved to a place of coherence by being in the animal's energy field.

In fact, studies by Rupert Sheldrake cited in his book *Dogs That Know When Their Owners Are Coming Home,* took a number of pet owners and put cameras in their houses to monitor the behaviour of the pets while the owners were away. Each day the owners were asked to stay away from the home for different periods of time, and indeed the owners never knew when they would be returning home. One remarkable thing noted by the researchers was that whenever the owner consciously decided they would go home (after instruction from the researcher) it was as though a telepathic message was sent to their pet animal and they knew the owner was coming home. This was evidenced by behaviour such as moving to sit at the front door or looking for the owner through the window. Since this behaviour mirrored the exact instant the owner decided to return home, the researchers concluded there was a form of emotional connection between the animal and its owner, enabling messages to be transported between them even though there was no visual communication.

So if animals so clearly help us gain connection to an inner part of ourselves why are there not Dog or Cat Assisted Coaching programmes? What makes the interaction with horses unique and therefore such great teachers? To answer this question we need to understand the basic instincts of horses. Unlike dogs and cats, horses are prey animals. To some extent they live in fear for their lives, never knowing where the next threat will come from and whose meal they may become. As a result, they have a highly developed radar that helps them be aware of all that surrounds them. They are what we refer to as present and grounded. They live moment to moment. They don't have the luxury of wondering what will happen next week because if they don't pay attention to what is happening right now they may well no longer be alive. Who knows where that sneaky mountain lion might be lurking, just ready to take them down? It is for this reason that horses live in a herd; they find safety in numbers. Just imagine how tiring it would be to be alone on the mountain range with danger all around you. How could you ever sleep or relax? You couldn't – because one relapse and failure to pay attention and you would be dead. This is why you rarely find horses alone in the wild. It just simply is not safe. The herd therefore not only offers safety and security but also companionship, a way of being in a community. So how is it that we rarely witness horses fighting with each other? It is because they have strict roles and responsibilities within the herd, everyone knows their place and role and this maintains order and unity.

The horse is also a flight animal. Unlike a predator that is a fight animal, when danger approaches a horse's natural instinct is to flee the danger, typically running up to a quarter of a mile or further to escape. So who decides where the herd flees to? Well, because of the strict hierarchy and order in the herd there is a leader, usually the lead mare (female horse), whose role it is to keep the herd safe and steer them to safety. The leader is always aware of any prevailing danger and ensures that the herd always has an escape route, a Plan B, should danger prevail. In the wild there is usually one male horse (stallion) with a herd of mares and the stallion works in conjunction with the lead mare of the herd to get everyone to safety as quickly as possible. There is an almost telepathic communication between the lead mare and the stallion so that they move in synchronicity. A great example of the innate communication that horses have between each other can be witnessed by the fact that when one horse notices danger and runs, the whole herd picks up on that energy and runs too. I remember hearing a story about a horse trainer who was explaining to his student how the horse could read her energy and that was why her riding lesson was not developing the way she wanted. To make his point the trainer grabbed a small pile of hay and lit a fire right near the girl's horse. The horse snorted and became wide-eyed in the presence of what he perceived as impending danger. However, what was remarkable was that the other horses in the barn, who were out of eyesight of this horse, picked up on his level of fear and anxiety and responded in kind by whinnying and running around looking for a way to escape the potential danger. I know from my own experience that my horses definitely pick up on group energy and respond in kind.

Scientists call this synchronistic movement *entrainment* and it is most evident when you watch a large flock of birds flying. Each bird knows exactly where to go – the path and trajectory to follow. You never see the birds crash into each other despite the fact they swoop and rise on the current. I remember being mesmerised watching a group of starlings flying over Otmoor RSPB Reserve near Oxford. There were literally thousands of birds and they traversed the sky en masse. In fact there were so many it looked like dark clouds in the sky. If you have never seen such a spectacle I urge you to watch out for one, but the concept is the same that can be seen in the inverse V formation that geese make when they fly.

So what is happening to cause all the birds to align in the same pattern? Entrainment was first discovered by a

clockmaker, Christiaan Huygens, in the 17th century. As
a clockmaker, Huygens accumulated quite a collection in
his studio and one night he noticed that all the pendulums
were swinging at the same time. Despite trying to
misalign the clock pendulums, they kept swinging back
in time once again. Although Huygens could not explain
this phenomenon at the time, later researchers figured out
that the largest pendulum clock electromagnetically had
the power to lull the others into alignment with it.

Many living and non-living things are affected by
entrainment and the flock of birds described earlier is just
one such example; another is shoals of fish. The largest
shoal recorded was witnessed off the New Jersey coastline
and it was estimated that it contained some 20 million
herrings. It is because of entrainment that your heart has
the power to control all the functions of the body – even
the brain. Entrainment enables the heart to set a rhythm
for the brain, but the brain can't do the same for the heart
as the heart has an electromagnetic (energy) field that is
5,000 times stronger than that of the brain and reaches
eight to ten feet from your body.

It is this ability to read our energy fields and connect to
our emotional intelligence that makes horses such powerful
teachers. They become a mirror for our own emotions,
helping us uncover parts of us that we would rather not
examine. They speak to our soul and ensure that we are
congruent and aligned. They break down the mask that
many of us wear in our daily lives and get to the real truth.
Horses provide us with immediate, 100% non-judgmental,
observable feedback, mirroring our internal reality. Living

in the 93% of the non-verbal world of communication, they are not impressed by position, status or power. They react to what is presented to them. They don't mind, let alone know, who the CEO of the business is, or the janitor; they just respond to what is happening to them in the here and now. This is why horses are such great teachers of leadership, communication and teamwork. They can show us how to build trust and become truly congruent and aligned. They teach us about authenticity and, by helping us connect with our emotional intelligence, they give us insight and perception by responding to our innermost emotions. Feelings, breathing, movement and posture give the horse a catalogue of information.

Today, our current conditioning often makes us ignore or question our innate instincts. In this time of complexity and rapid change it is essential to balance the vast technological resources and multitude of information that is readily available against instinct, self-awareness and intuition – our emotional intelligence. Working through horses enables us to connect to these often unused internal resources, and because it requires out of the box thinking, it is extremely metaphorical and memorable. Horses challenge us to connect and find our true self and so eloquently teach us that it is who we are that impacts how we perform in the boardroom and not what and who we know.

CHAPTER TWO

Leadership Begins With You

'Before you are a leader success is all about growing yourself. When you become a leader, success is all about growing others.'

Jack Welch

Leadership Begins With You

'Before you are a leader success is all about growing yourself. When you become a leader, success is all about growing others.'

Jack Welch

Leadership is that elusive quality that companies are looking for and yet, in my opinion, is so often lacking in organisations. Given the multitude of companies offering leadership training and the circa £3billion spent on external training annually in the UK, how come our companies are not some of the best performing in the world?

To my mind, leadership and management are too often confused. We expect managers to lead and yet leadership and management involve completely different skill sets. Indeed, the Peter Principal invariably plays out in organisations. The Peter Principal states that *'people are promoted to the level of their incompetency'.* This is why all too often people get promoted only to fail in their managerial role because what they really need are leadership skills.

So what is leadership? The Oxford Paperback Diction-ary defines a leader as *'one whose example is followed'*. Leadership has also been described as the work done by a leader who uses intelligence to succeed. Complete leader-ship starts with the vision and builds relationships with the people that share the vision and who will take on the task of achieving the vision. This differs from management which uses structures, rules and processes in order to control and predict results in a more stable situation.

Frank S. Greene notes that *'the success of management is seen in the industrial empires where people can be used interchangeably and as replaceable parts.'*

In order for any business to be successful it needs strong leaders and particularly so in this age of globalisation because whilst an individual might be able to mask their lack of leadership skills in a small organisation, in my experience once they have to manage across multiple locations they will be found out.

Great leadership involves developing a blend of vision, relationships and execution and as an organisation expands, the need for the leader to communicate that shared vision to a diverse set of people becomes paramount because unless the vision is shared, the organisation will never meet its goals. It will become like a ship bobbing up and down on the ocean with no clear direction of where it is heading and wonder why the business fails to move forwards.

There is a requirement for leaders to use their intelligence to inspire and influence change through strong leadership with people who see the benefit of being part of the future vision. This contrasts with traditional management approaches which seek to establish the structure and rules for engagement based on perceived economic benefit for both sides. External factors such as society, community, environment and political forces are typically not considered in developing these rules of engagement.

To my mind you cannot *learn* leadership because leadership *is* learning; however what we can do is enable leaders. We can enable leaders to learn about themselves. I am continually reminded of the words of John C. Maxwell who says that *'leadership is the ability to influence others'* and for me, this is so true. You simply cannot motivate others – people or horses – through force but rather you need to influence others and empower them to work alongside you in a partnership that is mutually beneficial to all parties.

There is one person, however, who is typically the most difficult person to lead and this is ourselves. This sentiment was summed up so well by international leadership speaker Mark Fritz at The Academy of Chief Executives Mastermind Group which I was attending when he said, "*The hardest person to lead is yourself.*" This is why I strongly believe you cannot learn leadership because it is not a theory or talent, it is about a way of being. To me leadership starts with self – leaderself. It is about understanding yourself and once you know and understand yourself then you can lead and influence others.

Linacre and Cann in *An Introduction to 3-Dimensional Leadership* define leadership as a state of being that involves all aspects of the human being – physical, mental, emotional and spiritual.

PHYSICAL	*The ability to manage your physical state, to be able to move from a state of potential stress or fear to a state of dynamic relaxation or 'flow' for optimal performance and the fulfilment of potential*
MENTAL	*To remain clear-sighted and rational without losing the ability to connect at the human level – to maintain a high level of emotional intelligence on the benefit of the greater good*
EMOTIONAL	*To acknowledge your emotional reactions, understand their purpose and integrate them into balanced, emotionally intelligent adult-to-adult interactions with those involved, in all circumstances, rooted in a clear perception of the present without regret of the past or fear of the future*
SPIRITUAL	*To know the purpose of your actions and how this purpose fulfils your personal sense of meaning and that of those your actions affect up to the level of your 'world'.*

Furthermore they go on to explain that *'leaders do, and enable other people to do, things that they have never done before in circumstances that have never previously existed. In other words, leaders act, and ACT stands for Awareness, Connection and Transformation.'* Leaders are aware and connected to themselves and to those they lead and the situation they find themselves in. The quality and awareness and the connection determines the level of transformation that can occur.

No one can dispute that we are living in unprecedented times. Never before have we experienced the current economic conditions following the financial crisis. We have no frame of reference with which we can benchmark and assess the future. Even the Governor of the Bank of England has openly stated that he has no idea what the situation will look like tomorrow, let alone next month or next year. There is a high level of uncertainty in our world today and that is making people scared. The culture of self-preservation in organisations has increased dramatically as people live in fear for their jobs and their economic security. Furthermore, following the spate of redundancies that occurred, many organisations are dysfunctional. They have people in roles that they are ill-equipped to fulfil and downsizing has meant new teams being formed with the express aim of achieving more with fewer resources. No wonder then, that this is perhaps one of the most challenging times we have ever seen for leaders of organisations. The pressure to deliver increased financial performance is significant, and aligning that with seeking to inspire a diverse group of people, each with their own agenda, we can clearly see that leadership today is not for the faint-hearted.

Before we move on, I want to make it very clear that leadership is not just about leading others. We have already discussed that leadership starts with self and you cannot lead others unless you can lead yourself. Some of you might argue that you never lead others; however I would like to propose that we are all obliged to lead. Leadership is a life skill that we need to develop in order to fulfil our potential. If you are a mother or father you lead your family; if you hold a position in the community you lead that group of people; but for me the most important person that we all need to lead is ourselves. All too often I hear people complaining about their life, about the lack of choices they can make and yet I'm here to tell you that we all have choices. We all have the ability to lead our own life and get the life we desire. Sure, it might be tough but leaders have that vision to see where they want to go and inspire others (or in this case themselves) to achieve it. So take hold of the reins and create the life you want by leading yourself to success.

Some of you might feel that what I am proposing is unfair and unjust and argue that you are stuck in situations that don't enable you to make choices and lead your life. I understand, I really do because I have been there. For years I had a very successful corporate career, I thought everything was wonderful and nothing could go wrong, and then the inevitable happened: the company for which I had worked for some 12 years made my role redundant. The specialised business unit that I ran for them was sold and, in the process, I found myself without a job. It was 2008, just before the financial crisis, and I was faced with some tough decisions. Did I seek to find another job in the City or did I do something different? It was in those moments of reflection that I realised that I had spent the last 20 years living someone else's life. Yes, I had a successful career and achieved many accolades, but I hadn't been doing what I really wanted to do, I had not been leading my own life. I had been living my parents' dream for me. Sure, it wasn't a bad dream, but since I was a teenager I had always wanted to work with horses and I remember being told at about the age of sixteen that I couldn't and that I had to get a proper job. So I did, and so began my journey into the corporate world. I never took the reins of my own life and, like many people, it took a significant event – my redundancy – to make me see what had been going on.

Today, it is my mantra to ensure that everyone has the knowledge and skills to help them lead their own lives because we only get one life and in my opinion it is our responsibility to live it to the full.

Types of Leadership Models

There is a myriad of information available on effective leadership styles and approaches and a plethora of companies offering leadership training and, like good horsemanship, there is no one solution that fits all. This is because, to my mind, leadership is an art not a science. At one end of the spectrum there are leaders who prefer to deal with emergencies and crises that threaten organisations, whilst at the other end of the spectrum there are leaders who by nature are more entrepreneurial in their approach, who relish the challenge of establishing new ventures and growing them rapidly. In between are leaders who prefer to work with existing organisations and energise and strengthen them over time. The approach taken will depend as much on the individual's personal traits as the external environment they find themselves in. As a consequence, the outcome will be very different. However, the common element to all effective leadership styles is that they create some form of vision, inspiration and motivation (VIM) for those impacted.

**Opposite: Adapted from 'The Varieties of VIM' by Max Landsberg –
the tools of leadership**

The Varieties of VIM

Leadership Type	Aspect of VIM		
	Vision of.....	Inspiration via....	Motivation through...
Grow Organisation Rapidly			
Entrepreneur *Creating New Ventures*	*The Challenge*	*Adventurous Spirit*	*Creatively Reallocating Resources*
Energise the Organisation			
Evangelist *Instilling Culture*	*Playing by the Rules*	*Missionary Zeal*	*Role Modelling*
Politician *Uniting the Team*	*Balance of Power*	*Wise Judgment*	*Reckoning of Power*
Strategist *Driving Strategic Initiatives*	*Collective Foresight*	*Compelling Logic*	*Key Performance Indicators*
Change Agent *Driving Operational Change*	*Order from Chaos*	*Challenge to Re-invent*	*Project Milestones* *External Benchmarks*
Deal with Emergencies			
Field Marshall *Respond to Crises*	*Victory*	*Call to Battle*	*Recognition*
Surgeon *Retrenching*	*Smaller but stronger and more adaptable*	*Salvation by own Hands*	*Performance Against Benchmarks*

To some extent, the style of leadership is determined by the nature of the challenge that the leader is drawn to. Few people can lead well in all situations and effective leaders know their strengths and weaknesses and when to draw on additional resources. When confronted with situations outside their comfort zone, effective leaders typically either:

- *Engage others who can complement their expertise*
- *View the situation as an opportunity to learn and extend their skills*

In many cases, a leader's limitations are linked to their beliefs and life philosophy – their mindset on how they see the world. This will affect, for example, the amount a leader hangs on to control versus delegates. What is apparent is that good leaders understand themselves and what their leadership limitations might be. They gain insight into their own drivers and so begins the journey of leading from the inside out.

Five Practices of Exemplary Leaders

So what are the practices that exemplary leaders demonstrate and that we should seek to emulate if we want success in our lives, whether personal or business? A study reported in the *Evening Standard* suggests that in today's ever-changing world the characteristics that employers are looking for in leaders include:

- *Ability to inspire and motivate – 36%*

- *High levels of emotional intelligence – 34%*

- *Ability to deal with people – 34%*

- *Natural leadership – 24%*

- *Trustworthiness – 22%*

- *A natural communicator – 22%*

- *Possessing vision – 22%*

- *Drive and ambition – 22%*

One leadership model that really resonates with me and can easily be modelled through working with horses is the Leadership Challenge designed by James M. Kouzes and Barry Z. Posner. In the Leadership Challenge, they identify five practices and ten commitments of leadership. However, before we examine these, it would be prudent to review how Kouzas and Posner define leadership. In their book *The Leadership Challenge,* they cite leadership as *"The art of mobilizing others to want to struggle for shared aspirations."* In this context, we can clearly see that leadership is all about relationships, which is something we will explore more fully in Chapter Eight. Over the course of 25 years, Kouzes and Posner have been collecting data from over three million respondents across 73 countries and what they have identified is that the main skills and practices of exemplary leaders can be summarised as:

Model the Way – set an example for the standards of excellence

- Find your voice and clarify your personal values
- Set the example by aligning actions with shared values

Inspire a Shared Vision – envision the future and enlist others

- Envision the future by imagining exciting and ennobling possibilities
- Enlist others in a common vision by appealing to shared expectations

Challenge the Process – search for ways to challenge the status quo

- Seek out opportunities for change, growth and improvement
- Experiment, take risks, generate small wins and learn from mistakes

Enable Others to Act – foster collaboration and build teams

- Foster collaboration by promoting co-operative goals and building trust
- Strengthen others by sharing power and discretion

Encourage the Heart - recognise contributions and celebrate accomplishments

- Recognise contributions by showing appreciation for individual excellence
- Celebrate the values and victories by creating a spirit of community

The trinity of leadership VIM – vision, inspiration, motivation – that we discussed earlier can also been seen to be at the heart of Kouzes and Posner's leadership model. So, leadership is all about setting and steering a course that ultimately leads to a result. The one thing that is so important to remember about leadership is that it always involves ACTION. Many people fail to start something because they don't feel that they can get off the starting block. They try to make the first action too large. Just chunk it down and take small steps, because the results that small cumulative steps can yield are amazing.

This reminds me of a saying that my mentor John Assaraf used to have: '*Inch by inch it's a cinch.*' Jeff Olsen in '*The Slight Edge*' uses a similar analogy. He describes a lily on a large pond. The lily looks tiny sitting on the surface water of the large pond, then, overnight, the lily multiplies; then on the next night, the lily multiples again, and then again on the fourth night. This sequence continues for 30 days until the pond is covered in beautiful, splendid flowers. The act of covering the entire pond in flowers would have seemed overwhelming for many, but chunking things down and doing one step and then repeating it consistently results in success way beyond what is anticipated. It is all due to the measure of consistency and tenacity applied.

A further attribute of leadership that we will examine is the fact that leadership is all about the journey and not the destination. Sure, as we have examined, leaders need to set the direction for the business, their own lives or whatever else they are involved in, but the reality is that they will always be off-course. Given that I fly a fair amount around the world, I remember being shocked to learn that an aeroplane spends 99% of its time off-course. So if you were flying from London to Los Angeles, a flight time of some 11 hours, it would mean that the plane is off-course for all but seven minutes of the entire journey. So how then do we get to our destination? The skill is that the pilot recognises when we are going off-course and then rectifies the situation. Tiny movements keep the plane on track and this is also how a good leader performs. They acknowledge when the business is moving off-track and then reset the course to ensure that they reach the destination. Certainly, like any journey, the plan you started out with needs to be flexible as the way may be blocked and you might need to seek an alternative route. With the clarity of knowing where you are going you can take the right action and inspire others to follow your lead by motivating them to achieve their goals.

Horses Always Ask - Who is Leading?

So how can Horse Assisted Coaching help people develop leadership skills? The answer lies in the fact that horses are always looking for a leader. As a prey animal, the horse always has to be aware of imminent danger or else he could end up as someone else's lunch. This means that a horse always has to be alert to any danger in his surroundings and also be in a position to run away should that danger present itself. To ensure that the horse can survive being a prey animal it has evolved so that its natural behaviour and physiology can keep it as protected as possible. This is why horses have eyes on the side of their head, as it gives them nearly 360 degree vision to see any approaching danger. They are also acutely aware of any changes in their environment, as this could herald the onset of approaching danger. The sense of community and camaraderie they gain from living in herds also helps keep horses safe. I'm sure you've heard of the idiom '*Safety in numbers*' – well, this is the premise that horses work from. The more of them that are together, the more eyes they have looking out for danger and so the safer they feel.

It is because of this desire to stay safe that a horse is always looking for a leader. Can you imagine living by yourself, never being able to rest and relax for fear of being attacked and eaten? This is a tiring place to be and the reason why a horse is willing to let us take up the leadership role with them. However, and this is a really big thing, we must prove to be a leader who can be trusted and who knows what they are doing. If we have no clarity or certainty and don't evoke a sense of trust from the horse then he will not let us lead him and he will take over the leadership position. You see, unlike people who might be quite polite when their boss is not being a clear, decisive leader, a horse has no option but to act, his life depends on it, whereas in a business we continue to tolerate poor leadership until such time that the leader is removed from that position – ironically often promoted to another position.

Different from humans, horses don't follow blindly, yet they are looking to be led. They cannot be coerced or influenced, they choose to follow. Horses have survived for thousands of years due to their ability to get along with, and depend upon, one another. They test each other to establish their position within the herd, deferring only to other horses they feel will keep them safe. In a world in which money, control and status are non-existent, horse leaders respond immediately to the thoughts, feelings and sometimes hidden agendas of those around them, and communicate with authority, purpose, authenticity and confidence – all without 'saying' a single word. Like some employees, horses can either be willing participants or resentful 'herd members', making them ideal partners for teaching self-leadership and teamwork.

Reflecting on my own leadership experiences, both in the barn and in the boardroom, I can now understand how, when and why different leadership approaches worked and why they did not. Specifically, I recall the time in 2002 when Andersen was taken over by Deloitte after the Enron scandal. It was a very difficult time for the entire company, including the team that I led. Our specialised hotel benchmarking research-offering was what I would describe as non-core to an accountancy firm like Deloitte, and we spent what felt like months wondering if our team would survive the acquisition or if we would be offered redundancy like many others in the organisation. Luckily our team survived the merger, but it was not without internal conflict throughout the struggle. As the team leader, I felt compelled to play the company line and encourage and motivate the team of the benefits of joining the new company; however, factions within the team felt that breaking away and establishing the team as a stand-alone business would be a preferable alternative. On reflection now, I did not manage that situation clearly and decisively. I did not lead from the front during this crisis time. I let myself get confused and conflicted by playing the company line and my desire to be an entrepreneur and lead my own business. No wonder then that disagreements broke out within the ranks and, in the end, a number of team members opted to leave. It was a real shame but for me a great leadership learning experience.

Klaus Hempfling, in his book *Dances with Horses*, has identified three leadership positions that can be adopted when leading a horse, or indeed any organisation. They work on the principle of pull-push leadership with certain styles being more effective in different circumstances.

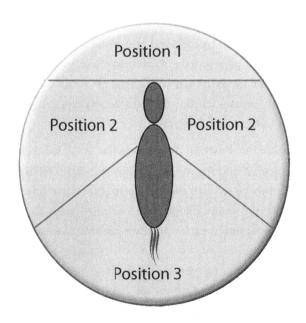

Leadership Position One is out front with the rest of the team members following. This leadership position is most effective in emergency situations when there is a need to take control because of some threat of danger. In this situation you just want people to follow and you don't want to negotiate on how and what you are doing – you just need people to trust you and act now as you prescribe. The challenge with maintaining this leadership position indefinitely is that for the leader it is a very tiring and lonely place to be – up front and alone. For team members, this type of leadership is equally challenging; constantly being told what to do becomes demoralising and team members quickly lack focus and engagement. It does not take much to get them off-track and they will wander off in their own direction, doing their own thing so that they can get some sense of being and self. I often observe this occurring in organisations and indeed have witnessed it first-hand; by becoming too controlling and micro-managing all aspects of the team, people have started to disconnect and lose interest and focus in their work. The net result is less than optimum results for the business as everyone is not all pulling in the same direction.

Leadership Position Three is what is called *Leading From Behind* and for me is the most powerful leadership position to be in. It relies on setting a course and then inspiring the team members to achieve this. It is an empowering and creative position for both the leader and the team members as everyone feels engaged, responsible and committed to achieving the goals. I have often heard it said that team members use less than 40% of their potential at work. *Leading From Behind* helps unlock that remaining 60% resulting in significant improvements in productivity, absenteeism, motivation and commitment from team members. The challenge for many leaders using this leadership style is that it involves setting the course and then allowing the team members to get there in their way – which might be a very different way from the one the leader envisaged. Continually nagging team members will not be successful and indeed may result in the team disappearing in another direction. This leadership position involves creating trust and empowering others.

Leadership Position Two is what might be described as a supportive leadership position. It is a position of true partnership and equality and has been likened to the time when you go down the pub with your team members. It is not a position that offers leadership and direction but is required to balance the other two leadership positions.

Within a herd of horses we see Leadership Positions One and Three used continually. Typically, in a herd of wild horses, you will find one stallion (a male horse) and then a band of mares (female horses). Within the band of mares there will be one horse that is the leader. If you get the opportunity to watch wild horses you will clearly be able to see the way that the lead mare and stallion work together to maintain the security and safety of the herd.

The stallion is typically found in Leadership Position Three, at the rear of the herd of horses. From here he can keep an eye out for approaching danger and also influence the direction of the herd by gently pushing them from behind. If he pushes too hard his herd of mares will disband. Unlike a business where employees often feel obligated to stay with their employer for income security, the stallion has no such control over his herd. Any inappropriate leadership and his herd of mares can just run away. He has no fences (or employment contracts!) to keep them in. The lead mare is typically found at the front of the herd, and her role is to find suitable grazing. She works in conjunction with the stallion, leading the herd to lush pastures and streams so they can stay nourished and refreshed. Whilst grazing, you will often find the lead mare adopting Leadership Position Two, hanging out with the herd and making sure everyone is alright.

Leadership Lessons from the Ranch

One of the most profound exercises that we undertake when people come to one of my *Unbridled Success* Retreats is to lead a horse around four poles located in different corners of the arena. For people that have never led a horse before, and experienced equine professionals, the results are astonishing. For some people the horses won't move at all, whilst in other cases the horses literally drag them around the arena. I remember last summer we were running this exercise in a field for a group of executives. The first person, who I shall call Jane, tried to lead the horse around the poles but kept finding the horse dragging her off to the most luscious grass it could find. Jane was getting really frustrated and said the exercise was too difficult because the horse just wanted to eat. So we changed positions and asked another client, Bill, to lead the horse around the poles. The result was completely different, with Bill leading the horse easily around the poles. So what was happening? Why did the horse respond in a completely different way to each person? Well, as we discussed the exercise, it transpired that Jane had been really unclear and uncertain about her ability to lead the horse. This uncertainty and lack of clarity had been felt by the horse who merely decided, 'If she can't be clear on her leadership then I'm going to lead her over to that grass.' Indeed, on reflection, Jane also admitted to feeling insecure in her role and this lack of clarity as to her role was causing her to lose personal confidence in her ability. Meanwhile, Bill had been really clear about what he wanted them both to achieve and the horse had felt compelled to follow him, even in the face of a better alternative in the form of lush grass. Armed with new insight, Jane was able to return to work and get some clarity on her role, which in turn enabled her to lead her team with more focus and direction.

Harness Your Authenticity

'The horse does not listen to our words,
our convincing tone or willing smile.
It listens only to that part of us that is authentic.'

Ariana Strozzi,
Horse Sense for the Leader Within

Harness Your Authenticity

'The horse does not listen to our words,
our convincing tone or willing smile.
It listens only to that part of us that is authentic.'

Ariana Strozzi, Horse Sense for the Leader Within

Horse Assisted Coaching requires us all – facilitator and client – to be true to ourselves and act with integrity, aligned to our values. For me, being authentic is more powerful than any amount of skills and qualifications. With authenticity comes a sense of genuineness and purpose, clarity and focus – all attributes that are quite often sadly lacking in our society. And why? Because the ego gets in the way. The ego is the mask that we wear to try and conform to society and live and act as others think we should. This famous quote from Hamlet sums up well the value of being authentic:

'This above all – to thine ownself be true;
And it must follow, as the night the day,
Thou canst not then be false to any man.'

Leadership depends on our ability to be in alignment, to be wholly congruent and therefore authentic. This is our natural state when we are feeling at our best, alive and decisive. Leadership does not mean knowing all the answers – you can decide not to decide, you can decide not to know, you can also decide what questions to ask. The point is that leadership is about making a decision, a choice, and sticking with it. All too often in organisations I come across people who dither around, they can't make a decision. Would this type of person inspire you to follow them? If you were a horse and your life depended upon this person could you trust them to make the right decision? I bet the answer is no. If your life depended on it you would rather follow someone who exuded confidence, clarity and certainty. Sure, they might make the wrong decision but at least they have made a decision and moved the organisation forward.

In her book *The Way of the Horse,* Linda Kohanov describes horses as *'authenticity meters'* and this is why they are such great teachers in a Horse Assisted Coaching session. As humans we have become experts at putting on masks to hide who we really are. In fact some of the people I have met have worn a mask for so long they don't really know who the true authentic real self is. As a result it is easy for them to delude both themselves and others that everything is as they want it in their life, when exactly the opposite is probably the truth.

So what are these masks and how do they come about?

To understand how and why people wear masks – whether consciously or unconsciously – it is useful to understand what our comfort zone is. According to Dr. Hans Christian Altmann our comfort zone is the area in which we feel comfortable. This comfort zone is determined by the environment and the experiences that we are brought up with and it is different for everyone. This is why one person is more than happy to fly in an aeroplane and another is not. Chances are the person happy to fly travelled on a plane many times during their formative childhood years, so going through an airport and getting on a plane is second nature to them. They are comfortable with the experience. If you have never been flying before then getting on an aeroplane may seem like you are entering the 'danger zone'. Within the danger zone can be feelings of guilt, hurt, inferiority and anxiety. You are just not happy here and this is why your neo-cortex brain tries to get you to stay in your comfort zone. The problem is that when you stay in your comfort zone and never leave it, it becomes smaller and smaller until you become stuck. This is what happens to many people. They get stuck in their comfort zone and consequently often become frustrated with life – much like if my horse had to stay in his 12' x 12' stable every day, he would become bored and very frustrated. It takes courage to leave your comfort zone but the rewards are immense, because every time you leave your comfort zone it becomes bigger and bigger and this enables you to become more creative and expansive and so reach your highest goals.

I feel that this poem by an unknown author so beautifully sums up the importance of, at times, leaving your comfort zone.

My Comfort Zone

*I used to have a comfort zone where I knew I
wouldn't fail.*
*The same four walls and busy work were really
more like jail.*
*I longed so much to do the things I'd never
done before,*
*But stayed inside my comfort zone and paced
the same old floor.*

I said it didn't matter that I wasn't doing much.
*I said I didn't care for things like commission checks
and such.*
I claimed to be so busy with the things inside the zone,
*But deep inside I longed for something special of
my own.*

I couldn't let my life go by just watching others win.
*I held my breath; I stepped outside and let the
change begin.*
*I took a step and with new strength I'd never
felt before,*
*I kissed my comfort zone goodbye and closed and
locked the door.*

If you're in a comfort zone, afraid to venture out,
*Remember that all winners were at one time filled
with doubt.*
*A step or two and words of praise can make your
dreams come true.*
*Reach for your future with a smile; success is there
for you!*

When we are born we are born pure and just as we really are – our true self is revealed. However, as we go through life we begin building up layers around the true self to protect us. Firstly, we build up a mask of who we fear we are, derived from the feelings and dangers that exist outside our comfort zone. We create a false negative image of ourselves which we feel we have to hide. So we create a second mask around our true self which is who we pretend to be. This is often who we think we should be to please those around us. The challenge is that it is often at odds with how our true, authentic self wants to be.

As we take off our first layer of masks we begin to create the possibility of intimacy. We begin to show ourselves, beyond the good-looking masks and into the darker masks: rage, control, prejudice, greed, fear, doubt, longing. Each of these has been carefully crafted from the material of our own lives and specifically from the fabric of our own wounding.

No wonder that we prefer to keep on the outer mask that makes others and ourselves feel that we are OK and therefore accepted into society. However, if we are brave enough to move beyond the false positive mask and beyond the more deeply shadowed false negative, we can re-find our True Self. This is the place where we are authentic, unique and soulful and not limited by story or defined by life's experiences, circumstances or other people! This is the place that horses can help us find immediately. They challenge our perception of the world and help us face up to the realities of life – because whilst wearing the mask might be comfortable, your whole being is misaligned and incongruent. In fact you are no longer leading your life, but rather the mask/persona that you have permitted to evolve is leading your life. It is a very sobering thought, as well as a real revelation, when someone realises that they have permission to be themselves and takes responsibility for their own life. Because, in fact, living behind a mask is draining; always having to do what is expected to maintain the mask takes up so much energy. You are living a lie.

Of course the great irony here is that many people are afraid of the truth of their self image. They falsely believe that if people know the truth about them they will be rejected, abandoned and lose control of their lives. This fear pervades people's lives under the axiom 'I'm not good enough' and it is this negative self-judgment that can limit a person's feeling of success. In 'Horse Sense for the Leader Within', Equine Guided Educator Arianne Strozzi reveals that, based on her experience, 98% of women she has coached live in a story that they are 'not good enough' and, through my own experiences, I would concur with this. Perversely, however, although many people profess to feeling 'not good enough' this is simply a story or mask to hide their real fear that they are more powerful than they could imagine. Marianne Williamson sums up this conundrum so well for me when she states:

> *"Our deepest fear is not that we are inadequate. Our deepest fear is that we are powerful beyond measure. It is our light, not our darkness, that most frightens us. We ask ourselves, "who am I to be brilliant, gorgeous, talented, and fabulous?" Actually, who are you not to be? You are a child of God. Your playing small doesn't serve the world. There's nothing enlightened about shrinking so that other people won't feel insecure around you. We are all meant to shine, as children do. We are born to make manifest the glory of God that is within us. It's not just in some of us, it's in everyone. And as we let our own light shine, we unconsciously give other people permission to do the same. As we are liberated from our own fear, our presence automatically liberates others."*

Horses help us close the gap between how we actually present ourselves to others as distinct from how we think we are being. As super-sensitive energy readers they are hard-wired to avoid predators and don't trust, respect or understand anything that is not authentic. When faced with inauthenticity a horse's natural instinct will be to run away – a response triggered by his flight response. At best he is likely to ignore you, as happened to Martin Clunes, the actor and co-incidentally the President of the British Horse Society, in the TV documentary *'HorsePower,'* when he experienced a Horse Assisted Therapy session in Arizona. During the session, the facilitator asked Martin Clunes to hang out with the horse and get the horse to connect with him. Now, Martin Clunes is a relatively experienced horseman and, despite his best attempts at getting the horse to connect with him, the horse just stayed away and drank water and ate hay. When the facilitator asked what was happening, Martin Clunes admitted that he just wanted the horse to acknowledge him and that he was upset that the horse was blatantly ignoring him. As these words were uttered, the horse raised its head and began to acknowledge Martin Clunes's presence – it was a breakthrough. And as Martin Clunes became clearer and more congruent in himself as to why he wanted the horse to connect with him, the horse obliged, eventually following him around like a dog on a leash. All the horse wanted was for Martin Clunes to lose his mask, acknowledge his need for recognition and take ownership of that emotion, and in doing so become more authentic.

CHAPTER FOUR

Listening To Lead

*'The art of communication is
the language of leadership.'*

James Humes

'Listening is the fuel for leadership.'

Mark Fritz

Listening To Lead

*'The art of communication is
the language of leadership.'*

James Humes

'Listening is the fuel for leadership.'

Mark Fritz

Communication is the life blood of any organisation/
relationship and yet time and time again I witness poor
communication taking place – whether it be the boss
failing to explain his vision for the company or the team
member too scared to communicate with their boss how
they are feeling. Just like Jane in an earlier chapter, our
inability to communicate leaves us in a state of turmoil,
uncertain about what is happening and this invariably
leads to stress and anxiety. And it is not just we who
are affected; our friends, family and work colleagues
are also impacted by the troubled state we get ourselves
into because communication is about so much more
than just words.

I'll never forget the first time that the work of UCLA
psychology professor Albert Mehrabian was shared with
me. It was such an eye-opener for me and helped me

understand why in the past some of my team members had described me as 'scary'. I had just never understood why some people viewed me as scary because up to that point I had misguidedly believed I was one of the most approachable and friendly people in the office. What Albert Mehrabian discovered was that face-to-face communication can be broken down into three components:

- *Words*
- *Tone of Voice*
- *Body Language*

And when verbal and non-verbal messages are not consistent, what people see us do and the tone we use can far outweigh the words that we say. Furthermore he noted that when feelings and attitudes are being communicated then:

- *What we say accounts for only 7% of what is believed*
- *The way we say it accounts for 38%*
- *What others see accounts for 55%*

Amazingly, this means that more than 90% of the impression that we usually convey has nothing to do with what we actually say and this is why great leaders understand the importance of listening. For me, the realisation that it was not what I said that was important was somewhat damning and depressing, because up to that point I had been spending hours figuring out the best things to say to my team members. In that instant I realised it was not so much what I said that was important but how I said it. My body language was vital. Not surprising then, that some of my team thought I was scary. On reflection, my body language was like a coiled spring, ready to be unleashed as I rushed around the office, always busy doing something, never stopping, focused on my own goals and failing to see the impact my actions were having on others.

The realisation that words are not everything has been a real breakthrough, especially when it comes to any type of professional speaking or training. It has been documented that more people are scared of standing up and addressing a crowd (public speaking) than dying. How sad is that? Speakers spend hours and hours preparing their material, focusing on the words and content, and yet at the end of the day the stark realisation is that words and content are only one aspect of the presentation. The larger and more important factor to focus on is the delivery. Body language and tone of voice will have a much larger impact – 93% – than the words that we speak. This is one of the reasons why video channels such as YouTube have proliferated in recent years. YouTube is now the second most popular online search-engine after Google.

So why has video become so popular? The reason is that video enables people to connect more closely with the message being delivered because all the senses are being used – auditory, visual and kinaesthetic. The message has more meaning and substance and is not as dull as mere words. I'm sure you have all experienced times when you have written something – maybe an email at work – only to find the recipient is upset with you, and that was never the intent. With only the words to go on, the recipient overlays their own interpretation on to the message and, in seconds, a perfectly innocent comment has become the cause of great hurt. This situation is being compounded by the use of texts, tweets and Facebook, where a limited number of characters and the use of symbols only serve to further hamper communication.

So what is it that horses can teach us about communication and, indeed, how can we communicate with them? Well, it is the reason that communication is only 7% words that we can engage in interspecies communication. Horses are master communicators. As prey animals they live in the present moment, with their acute perception and survival instincts perfected over millennia. They rely on and look to the alpha horse to protect them and make the right decisions whenever the herd is in danger and requires leadership. Horses are sociable animals with distinct personalities. They are experts at non-verbal communication and help us improve our communication skills by reacting to human responses and body language. Sensitive animals, highly intuitive, they react to the smallest changes and stimuli in their environment.

Horses as Teachers of Body Language

What horses help us to understand is how our body language influences others. I remember back in 2004 when I was working full time in London and had my first horse, I never saw him apart from at weekends, as making the near two-hour journey to and from London daily meant I never had time to see him during the week. It was dark when I left home in the morning and dark when I got home at night. So weekends were a precious time for me, a time to ride my horse but also to get all the household chores done for the week: cleaning, ironing, shopping – my weekends were packed and I lived on a tight military schedule. Typically, I allocated a two-hour slot on both weekend days to go and get my horse Toby in from the field where he was kept, groom him, ride him and then turn him out again. For a whole summer I was never able to catch my horse!! I didn't understand at the time, but if you are grazing in a field full of grass and someone approaches you marching full speed ahead, high energy, would you want to stay around and engage with them? I think not and my horse Toby thought the same. It would take many months for me to realise that I needed to lower my energy level and make my body language softer and more inviting before my horse would consider engaging with me.

In fact, what I was doing was being 'scary', just like I was at work. The difference was that Toby told me in no uncertain terms what he thought about my body language by running away, something my team members were less inclined to do. Those lessons he taught me were invaluable in how to have a more approachable manner with people and situations, because if you are not approachable, no one will engage with you and you will be unable to communicate and connect effectively. This is the power of Horse Assisted Coaching as you get the unbiased, immediate feedback from the horse. He does not know, or indeed care, what position you hold in your work herd, he reacts only to the situation put before him and the energy, intention and body language that you present. There is no pretence here. Unlike team members who might be reticent to speak out, the horse just reacts to what you present him with – but beware, the outcome might not be to your taste!

So, once we understand the limitations of words in communication, what can we do to help us communicate more effectively? In his book *Everyone Communicates, Few Connect,* John C. Maxwell cites the work of his mentor Howard Hendricks, who suggests that communication has three essential components: the intellectual, the emotional and the volitional. In other words, when we try to communicate we must include:

- **Thought:** *something we know*
- **Emotion:** *something we feel*
- **Action:** *something we do*

John Maxwell believes that failure to include any of these three components results in a breakdown of communication and hence a disconnection from people. Specifically, he states the different ways that the breakdown will occur if you try to communicate without these elements:

- **Dispassionate** – *something you know but do not feel*
- **Theoretical** – *something you know but others do not*
- **Unfounded** – *something you feel but do not know*
- **Hypo-critical** – *something you feel but do not do*
- **Presumptuous** – *something you do but do not know*
- **Mechanical** – *something you do but do not feel*

When one or all of the components are missing, it is exhausting for the communicator, whereas when all three components – thought, emotion and action – are included, the communication is effortless and has conviction, passion and credibility. I'm sure you can all recall times when you have been in training sessions and you just cannot connect with the trainer. Those days seem the most boring and pointless ever and invariably I get incredibly tired. Then on other days I just can't get enough of the trainer and the days rush past and learning seems no effort at all. It is the same for the trainer or the professional speaker – connect with your audience and the time speeds away, fail to connect and it will feel like the longest training session or professional speaking engagement ever.

It is how you present yourself (your body language) and the tonality of your voice that keeps others engaged. I have recently become a member of Andy Harrington's Professional Speakers Academy and much of what we learn in this programme is about how to improve your body posture and voice tonality. For example, there are three types of tonality – visual, auditory, kinaesthetic (VAK) and at least five different gestures, and it is imperative that as a professional speaker you use all these techniques. Why? Because different people relate to different types of sounds and body language. The combined use of all of these skills helps rapidly build rapport with your audience and so helps them learn and understand the material that you are presenting. It is much the same communicating with horses; you need to use the right tone, approach and body language to get the result that you intend. I use the term *intend* quite specifically here, but often what I experience and observe with my clients is what they say they want and what they actually want are two quite different things.

A great example of this happened with a client we shall call Zoe; she came to work with me ostensibly to work through some very challenging times she had experienced in her marriage that left her with low self-esteem and confidence. We walked out into the paddock and Zoe introduced herself to my herd of horses and I then asked her which horse she would like to work with. She opted to work with my young filly Bracken. I don't know why but I just knew Zoe would choose this horse. I was in a dilemma because Bracken had not done much of this work beforehand but I trusted her implicitly and knew that, if Zoe had selected her, Bracken would be able to share with Zoe the lessons she needed to learn. What was interesting to me was that Bracken's own past contained some remarkable parallels to Zoe's. Outwardly friendly and chatty, a bit 'it's all about me' on the surface, in fact, Bracken was quite shy and scared. She hadn't had a great start to her life before she came to me and, like Zoe, needed to learn how to be more confident and trusting.

We went into the arena and I asked Zoe to move Bracken around the arena using a flag. To begin with, Zoe just waved the flag and Bracken just stood there, fixed to the spot. This lack of activity from Bracken was contrary to her usual behaviour and so Zoe and I begun to chat about what was happening. It transpired that Zoe selected Bracken because she reminded her of her young son – a bit cheeky and mischievous. Since the split from her husband, Zoe felt that the connection with her son had disintegrated and so she was conflicted, wanting to move Bracken (who to her represented her young son) away from her whilst at the same time needing and wanting the connection. Zoe's actions and intentions were misaligned as physically, she was waving the flag asking Bracken to move, but emotionally and energetically, she wanted the pony to stay close to her. Horses are so sensitive and can read our body language and intentions and if these are not aligned (that is to say, they are incongruent) they simply will not respond, just as Bracken did not.

To me even now, having seen this happen on numerous occasions, it amazes me how we can delude ourselves that we want something that we really don't. Our emotional brain has the ability to rationalise so much for us that we can become disconnected from the heart and what we truly want to achieve. Horses provide us with a crystal-clear mirror showing us what is truly going on in our lives. They can read our heartfelt desires even when we can't and help us confront those demons that we hide away from. There is no escape from the laser insight that a horse can give us about how we feel because as '*authenticity meters*' of the soul, they read our inner being and help connect us to the greatness within each and every one of us.

CHAPTER FIVE

Connect To Succeed

'You can have brilliant ideas, but if you can't get them across, your ideas won't go anywhere.'

Lee Iacocca

Connect To Succeed

'You can have brilliant ideas, but if you can't get them across, your ideas won't go anywhere.'

Lee Iacocca

Whilst good communication and leadership are all important, both in business and when working with horses, it is connection that forms the essential foundation of this triage. This is because if you can connect with others at all levels – one on one, in groups and with an audience – then relationships are stronger, your sense of community and belonging improves, your ability to create teamwork increases and your influence and productivity expands. So what do we mean by connection? John C. Maxwell defines connection as:

 "The ability to identify with people and relate to them in a way that increases your influence with them."

The benefits of learning to communicate and connect are immense: better personal and family relationships, better business relationships and in general a better experience of life. According to the Harvard Business Review, *'The*

number one criterion for advancement and promotion for professionals is an ability to communicate effectively' which translates into developing better connections with the people around you. It is also important to remember that you need to be able to connect with yourself as well because if you cannot be honest with yourself and communicate freely with yourself about your needs and desires, then you clearly can't articulate this to others. I have witnessed this on many occasions when people have needed or wanted help from others but have been unclear as to what it may be. When we don't know what we want ourselves then we can't articulate this to others.

I was fortunate recently to meet a lovely lady called Nadine Honeybone. After the birth of her first son, Nadine discovered that he was autistic. Although knowing nothing about autism, Nadine committed to finding out more about this disability and also helping others who found themselves in a similar plight. She has now formed The Autism Directory which provides help and support to other families with autistic children. As a result of the circumstances she found herself in, Nadine connected to her true self and in doing so become very clear on what she wanted to do. She connected to her purpose and, when you listen to Nadine speak, you cannot help but be inspired by her passion and enthusiasm for helping others. Nadine is very clear on what message and support she wants to offer others and as a result she is great connector.

Nadine has shown me that connecting is never about me; it is about the people who you connect with. As Zig Ziglar states: "*If you first help people get what they want, they will help you get what you want.*" Nadine selflessly helps other parents of autistic children and has learned the golden rule that when you are trying to connect with others it is not about you, it is about them. So if you want to connect with others, you have to get over yourself. You have to focus on others and not yourself. This is equally true in business. As a leader you cannot be self-centred but rather you need to focus on the needs of your team members and customers because you won't advance far in business if you cannot work through others. Successful people in business understand that success comes from connecting with others.

I personally have learned a number of lessons – both in business and from the horses – that echo this sentiment time and time again. A classic example of this happened recently at the yard where I keep my horses. One of the horses had got sick and had potentially infected the other horses in the yard. I could have got upset by this and angry at the person involved but what would that have achieved? Instead I tried to be supportive and offer solutions that would minimise the problem. The net result was that we managed to mitigate all the risks involved and none of the other horses got sick. So by connecting and helping my friend with her dilemma, I also managed to ensure that all my horses stayed healthy.

Laura Surovik, a trainer at Sea World in Orlando, Florida, works with Killer Whales and she sums up very succinctly the fact that connection is all about caring for others when she writes:

> *"I have been a trainer for twenty-four years and have been "connecting" and teaching others how to connect with Shamu for many years. Shamu has been one of my greatest teachers too. When you look into a Killer Whale's eyes, you realise that it is not about you. It can't be. The connection is made when they know that you are there for them – it's all about building trust through a loving, caring relationship. You must be sincere and worthy of being followed to connect and build a relationship with the ocean's top predator."*

Connecting with others – whether humans or horses – by caring for them creates amazing relationships and results. During our Horse Assisted Coaching sessions we invariably get people to stand in the centre of the round pen with a horse and 'breathe' with them. We ask the client to put one of their hands on the base of the horse's neck and the other on the horse's chest, in the heart area, and to synchronise their breathing with the horse. This simple exercise has a profound effect on people and often as they think about the horse, it brings up other memories for them.

We recently had a lady (we shall call her Susan) attending one of our Taster Experience Workshops. We asked Susan to introduce herself to the horses in the herd and then choose one horse that she would like to stand and breathe with. Susan chose an elderly mare called Olive. Olive was the matriarch of the herd and nearly 30 years old (which in horse years is pretty old). As Susan stood in the arena with Olive she began to cry with tears streaming down her face. We let Susan stand there with Olive as she sobbed uncontrollably and Olive, as if knowing something was wrong, bent her neck round almost encapsulating Susan in a big hug. Susan later shared with me that standing with Olive had brought back memories for her of her mother who had passed away just a few months previously. Susan also shared that she had never really grieved for her mother and it was as if Olive gave her permission to grieve now. It was a very moving experience.

Four Components of Connection

To succeed when connecting with others, more than words are required. In fact, connection happens on four levels – visually, intellectually, emotionally and verbally.

1. *Connecting Visually – What You See*

Research has shown that, as a species, we remember 50% of what we see but less than 20% of what we hear, whilst we retain 80% of what we experience. This is why action-based or experiential learning is such a cost-effective and valuable tool for helping people to learn new skills and methodologies. This is also why, as we highlighted earlier, YouTube has become the second largest search engine after Google with some 500,000 million users.

We now live in a visual age and people can perceive a lot in seven seconds. This is why it is imperative that any good public speaker immediately engages their audience when they walk on stage. To this end I have always been taught to open my presentations with an engaging question which will elicit a positive 'yes' response from the audience.

Andy Harrington, the UK's leading authority on the psychology of success, often starts many of his presentations by asking his audience, "I guess most of you are here because you want to make more money?" He then gets the audience to raise their hand if they are there because they want more money. By asking this question, and given the subject matter of his presentation, there is a huge likelihood that the audience will answer positively and as the group responds positively he creates social proof – that collective need that everyone desires the same outcome as you. The result is that the audience immediately connects with Andy as they have some shared values, and the audience also feels connected to other audience members as they all have something in common. In fact, Andy is one of the most charismatic, inspiring presenters I have come across in the field of Personal Development and this stems predominantly from his ability to quickly build rapport with his audience.

The seven-second rule is also why it is so important to make a great first impression. I don't know about you, but when I was working in London and someone came in for an interview or a business meeting I often found myself making a snap judgment about them, often based on what they looked like. I'm ashamed to confess that I fell into this trap very early on in my corporate career when I was interviewing candidates for a researcher position in my team. One candidate, a young man, turned up for the interview impeccably dressed; however his suit was a deep plum colour which was totally at odds with the navy, grey and black suits that the men in my office wore. The fact that this candidate was wearing a plum-coloured suit meant that I just could not take him seriously, and so, instantly, I deemed him an unacceptable candidate. I can still recall now having to go through the entire interview process with him knowing that I could never hire him. It was the longest hour of my life as I simply could not connect with him. So for this reason it is important to eliminate personal distractions and ensure that your dress matches someone else's expectations.

The other factor to consider is how much our facial expressions give away about how we feel about something. They convey a message even when we think we are hiding that message. Indeed, a poker face conveys a message of detachment, whilst roaming eyes when chatting with someone at a cocktail party invariably hint at the fact that you are disinterested in the person you are talking to and looking for someone else to connect with.

When I worked at Andersen and Deloitte, I was privileged to attend a number of cocktail parties with the hospitality industry's leading influencers. I will never forget there was one particular gentleman (who shall remain nameless) who had an uncanny ability to make most people to whom he spoke feel inferior. Whenever you spoke to him you could see he was always searching the room looking for someone more important to speak to. Consequently, he was always detached from the conversation and this made it very difficult to connect with him.

On reflection, I also unwittingly did a great job of this whilst working in London. Our office, which was open plan, was laid out so that my back was to the rest of the team. Invariably I was in the office before anyone else so when my team members came into work all they saw was my back. If they said "good morning" I would respond but continue to look away from them, working at my desk. They must have thought I was so rude and very uncaring.

I also remember a time when I was in my early twenties when my facial expressions caused me to forfeit a great opportunity that was presented to me. I remember being at dinner in a fine London restaurant with my boyfriend Howard Flannery and a gentleman called Chuck Feeney, who my boyfriend was working for. At that time we both worked in the hotel industry and Chuck owned a chain of hotels. Over dinner, completely unexpectedly, he offered Howard and me the opportunity to go and work for him in Spain. As I had just landed a great job at Gleneagles Hotel, a new job opportunity was the last thing on my mind. Consequently, I'll never forget the complete look of shock and horror that came over my face. I was completely unprepared and instinctively reacted in what was perceived as a negative way. Needless to say, that opportunity never presented itself again which was a shame because, on reflection, it could have been a great experience.

Other visual factors to consider include your physiology (posture) and also your environment. Tony Robbins in his *Unleash the Power Within* seminars talks a lot about how your posture affects your state and how by changing your posture you can change your emotional state. In his strategic intervention sessions, Tony Robbins often helps people who are suffering from depression to change state by asking them about their best sexual experience. People are generally so shocked at being asked this question that they laugh and then smile, as their physiology and posture changes. Their emotional state is now no longer that of a depressed person.

Similarly, the environment can have a massive effect on your ability to connect with people. Few speakers connect with an audience well if they stand behind a podium. Likewise, the most successful businessmen don't sit behind their desk for an important meeting but instead, sit adjacent to their client so they can remove any barriers to communication and therefore connect more effectively.

2. Connecting Intellectually – What People Understand

To connect most effectively intellectually, you need to understand both yourself and your subject matter. I'm sure you have all come across people who profess to be passionate about a subject but it simply does not come over that way. Invariably they are delivering someone else's message and so it lacks congruency and authenticity with them. This is why it is imperative that the CEO of a company can connect with his lieutenants and so share with them his vision for the company to enable them to convey the message to their team members with the same passion and conviction. The CEO needs to be clear on the 'What's in it for me' so that the lieutenants can buy into and embrace the vision. If they don't, when the vision is shared somewhere down the line, it will lack substance and credibility.

This is where horses are excellent at giving us feedback. They just hate incongruence and inauthenticity and so immediately respond to what they observe. I remember reading a great example of this happening when a lady was working in a round pen with a horse. As the woman stated her declaration for her life and asked the horse to move forward it just stood there, almost transfixed on the spot. The lady re-stated her intention, which was to move to Seattle and enjoy her new job. The horse continued to stand still, failing to move. After a while, the facilitator asked the lady what was happening and she recounted that, in fact, she did not really want to move to Seattle for this new high-flying job. This was not really her life intention at all; it was the life intention that everyone else had for her. What she really wanted to do was stay at home and look after her children. As the lady became congruent and connected emotionally with what she wanted, the horse began to move, reflecting the harmony that the lady was now experiencing in her body.

3. Connecting Emotionally – What People Feel

When connecting with people it is important you let them know how you feel and also recognise how they might feel. You need to appeal to the heart of your audience and, whilst rational reasons might support a buying decision, it is usually an emotional decision that drives it. As the adage goes:

Facts Tell – Stories Sell
Emotion Buys – Logic Justifies

People connect with your attitude and if they like your attitude and know, like and trust you, then a sale is more likely to occur. People are attracted and connect to the confidence of the speaker or the salesperson. Just think about it. If you are in business and you need to select between two companies to provide, say, consultancy services to your business, which would you choose? Would you choose the company that had the best methodology and service levels but team members who were uninspiring and boring, or would you choose the company with maybe slightly lesser credentials but who took time to understand the needs of your business?

Back in the mid 1990s I was working for a boutique hotel consultancy firm. The partners had sought to buy out the business from the mid-sized accountancy firm that owned it; however, for a number of reasons the deal had fallen apart at the final hour. The result was that some of the key partners who I had worked for over the last three years decided it was only appropriate to leave the business and one of these was my then mentor Frank Croston. Frank moved to Andersen and then encouraged me to join him and set up a hotel research team. It was an opportunity not to be missed. The remaining partners at my current firm also encouraged me to stay with them and in fact, offered me considerably more money to stay there. In the end, however, the decision was not about money, it came down to my ability to connect and trust the people I would be working for. The partners at my current firm gave me loads of intellectual reasons why I should stay with them, but their words lacked passion and conviction. They did not appeal to my heart and so I jumped ship and moved to Andersen which was a decision I never regretted.

Doc Childre and Bruce Cryer of the Institute of Heart Math in their book *From Chaos to Coherence,* explain how being in the right heartfelt state can have a significant impact on the performance of a company's salesforce. Since the first impression that a buyer has of a salesperson is usually an emotional one – feelings of discomfort and distrust or of security and comfort – the salesperson's emotional coherence greatly impacts the interaction. Rightly or wrongly, the buyer forms an opinion of the salesperson at high speed and if the salesperson seems insincere, pushy or emotionally unstable then the buyer often has reservations about making the purchase. I'm sure you have all heard the old axiom 'nothing is as ineffective as a desperate salesperson'. Conversely, increased coherence and emotional stability in the salesperson fosters greater respect and trust in the buyer and provides them with confidence. The outcome is that a sale is more likely.

4. Connecting Verbally – What People Hear

Even though words only make up 7% of the communication matrix, the words we choose to use are very important. You only have to look at all the quotations still used today to realise this. Many of Shakespeare's phrases are still in use some four hundred years after his death. Likewise, listen to something like Martin Luther King's speech or Nelson Mandela's and you can't help but be inspired by the words. Words are the currency of ideas and, despite comprising only a small part of the communication matrix, they have the power to change the world. As Mark Twain observed, *"The difference between the almost right word and the right word is really a large matter – it's the difference between the lightening bug and the lightening."*

When coaching, training and presenting, I always seek to use positive words and phrases that will instil confidence in my audience and are memorable and punchy. However, as well as considering the words, it is also important to realise that how we say something has an impact. People derive a lot from the tone, inflection, timing, volume and pacing of our words. All these factors can influence whether someone connects with or disconnects from you.

Connection therefore is a pivotal part of successful communication and leadership and what horses teach us is that this connection must come from a place of authenticity. Your message and style must be your own or else you simply become someone else's parrot, squawking out what you think you should say rather than what you believe. If this comes up then you are certainly not taking responsibility and leading your own life; so how can you expect to be a great leader for others?

Remember the words of Ralph Waldo Emerson who said, *"What you are speaks so loudly that I can't hear what you say."*

Trust The Process and Your Intuition

'Trust is the biggest business commodity of the decade. Without trust relationships and businesses falter.'

Stephen R. Covey

CHAPTER SIX

Trust The Process
and Your Intuition

'Trust is the biggest business commodity
of the decade. Without trust relationships
and businesses falter.'

Stephen R. Covey

In today's networked world, trust has become the new currency – the critical competency for individuals, teams, organisations and even countries. Trust impacts every situation – personal, business and even your relationship with a horse. Robert A. McDonald, Chairman, President and CEO, The Procter & Gamble Company, when referring to Stephen R. Covey's book *Smart Trust,* states: *"It is both a mindset and a toolbox for 21st-century leadership".* Therefore, trust clearly is an important commodity that cannot be overlooked in businesses and relationships today.

John C. Maxwell in '*The 21 Irrefutable Laws of Leadership*' defines that Law Six – The Law of Solid Ground – is based on the premise that Trust is the Foundation of Leadership. It is the glue that holds relationships and organisations together. Leaders cannot break trust with people and continue to influence them; it simply does not happen. This is much the same with horses. Horses thrive on a trusting relationship with their handler/owner and once that trust is breached it takes a long time to repair, and in some instances is never repairable. A lack of trust is prevalent in business today as employees no longer trust employers to look after them. Long gone are the days when people had a job for life. Today organisations will quickly downsize when economic conditions get tough. There is no loyalty from employees to employers or vice versa. The recent financial crisis of 2008/9 has made more and more people distrustful of the banking institutions, as well as the government's ability to handle these situations. Witness too the growing mistrust between couples in relationships, resulting in some of the highest divorce rates in England and Wales that we have ever seen.

A great analogy to describe how trust is measured is to compare it to money. Each time you make a good leadership decision you build trust and so earn more money. Conversely, each time you make poor leadership decisions you pay out some of your money as trust is eroded. All leaders start with a certain amount of money in their pockets or piggy bank; how they act determines whether that pile of money grows or becomes depleted. If a leader keeps making bad decisions then eventually the pile of money disappears – they have run out of trust with those they influence and it doesn't matter whether the last blunder is big or small, it will be the straw that breaks the camel's back, so to speak, and the reason that mistrust develops in the organisation.

So how does a leader build trust in those that follow him, and also in himself, since good leadership involves leading from the inside out? The answer lies in consistently exemplifying:

- *Competence*
- *Connection*
- *Character*

Ralph Waldo Emerson states that "*Self trust is the first secret to success*", because just as you can't lead others until you can lead yourself, you can't trust others until you can trust yourself. In his book *The Speed of Trust*, Stephen R. Covey describes the first wave of trust as self–trust. It is all about being credible and developing integrity, intent, capabilities and results that make you believable, both to yourself and others.

Building trust with yourself starts with the small things in life. Like making an appointment with your wife for dinner and then making sure that you follow through on it, despite an urgent commitment coming up at work. Being on time to meet friends and not finding excuses for cancelling just because you don't feel up to it. Putting appointments in your diary and then making sure you keep them.

I know from my own experience how difficult it can be sometimes to keep those appointments with myself. It is so easy when the alarm goes off in the morning to find an excuse for not exercising today, or getting up and writing my book. Over these last few months it has taken me courage and determination to set aside time to write.

Sure, there is always something else pressing to do, but I know that every time I fail to keep these commitments to myself I notice my self-esteem and self-confidence slipping away. I fail to inspire others to believe in me and so trust in my abilities. The net result is that my business suffers. Though we all know it intuitively, research validates that a person's self-confidence affects their performance. This is why Jack Welch of GE always felt so strongly that *"Building self confidence in others is a huge part of leadership."* Furthermore, a lack of self-trust also determines our ability to trust others. In the words of Cardinal de Retz, *"A man who doesn't trust himself can never really trust anyone else."*

Just like the earlier analogy of trust being measured by money, it is the small things we do that ultimately impact how people trust us. We might not realise it, but telling a white lie here and failing to keep an appointment there, all impact the credibility we have. And if we are not credible then we are not trustworthy; people simply don't believe that we will follow through on our actions. We lack integrity. When working and being around horses it is essential that we show up as trustworthy because if we are not trustworthy we cannot lead and we know that horses are always looking for a leader.

Time and time again on my *Unbridled Success* retreats I come across people who simply lack credibility in the horse's eyes. One of the exercises that I get clients to do is to move a horse out of their personal space and it is amazing how many people can't do this. They make the request to the horse to move by waving their arms or swishing a light reed (a long piece of willow) and then when the horse fails to move, they quit. They fail to follow through when their instructions are ignored. The result is that the next time the horse is asked to move he stands still or, even worse, backs into the person. The horse simply does not believe that the person really wants them to move – the person lacks credibility.

My recent personal experience with Bracken, a young horse in my herd, demonstrates perfectly the impact that failing to be consistent and credible in your actions can have. Bracken came to me having been found abandoned. She was weak and frail and quite afraid of humans. Over the following few months I cared for her and we developed a great bond and friendship. She trusted me implicitly to keep her safe as I never did anything to harm her. However, as happens in all great relationships, she gradually began to lose respect for me. Why was this? Well it crept up on me so slowly I barely noticed, but on reflection I started to make requests to her, like moving out of my space, and if she failed to move I gave her the benefit of the doubt. She was young and just starting her training. However, what was happening was that Bracken started to think that I was not credible. If I made a request and she did not oblige it wouldn't matter as I would just quit. Quickly, Bracken began to lose trust in my abilities and therefore my leadership as well. When I realised what I had done I was mortified, as I continually coach my clients in the importance of following through on their actions and being credible and yet, there I was ably demonstrating how to do exactly what I tell others not to do. It was an *Accelerated*

Horse Awareness™ (AHA) moment of huge proportions and a great lesson for me on how easy it is for us to quit before we get the outcome we desire.

I wonder how many leaders in business quit before they get the outcome they desire? The ramifications are huge as not only do you fail to complete the task you are undertaking, you lose credibility with your peers and ultimately, therefore, their trust and respect. And yet often, in my experience, leaders quit before they get the outcome they desire because they become influenced by others and lack trust in their own decisions.

Reflecting on my own career, I was guilty of this when I first became a leader. I'd ask people to undertake tasks and then because I lacked self-confidence in my abilities, I would allow myself to be persuaded that my decision was not a good one. I'd then back down, losing both trust and credibility with my team members. Conversely, when I was absolutely certain that I had made the right decision, even in the face of adversity, I was able to engage my team members and get the project completed super-fast. An example of this happened back in 1999 when we launched the first ever online internet-based benchmarking platform for the hospitality industry. At that time Andersen were pioneers in developing online communities for clients and had a platform called *KnowledgeSpace.* The company policy was that all online industry platforms should have the domain name **www.knowledgespace. com/industryname**. Well, I felt that this domain name conveyed no sense of community feel to our audience who were all hotel professionals. So I flouted convention and named our online community **www.HotelBenchmark. com**. I must admit there were some agonising days once we had unveiled the site when we thought it might be closed down for not being company compliant, but in the end, good sense prevailed and HotelBenchmark remained the undisputed industry market leader for nearly a decade until it was sold in 2008.

I observe this pattern of inconsistent behaviour happening a lot between parents and their children. The child does something that the parent doesn't want, like taking some sweets out of the jar, and the parent tells the child "No." The child continues to unwrap the sweet and the parent continues to tell the child to put the sweet back. Then a relative/friend or another adult says, "It's OKAY, little Johnny can eat that." Immediately the parent has lost all credibility with the child and the child rapidly begins to learn that No does not really mean No. A better solution would have been to remove the sweet from the child and then move the child to an area away from the sweet. Initially, being this clear, assertive and credible in your communication takes time, effort, commitment and follow-through, but in the long term it pays dividends as you no longer have to repeat yourself and your child learns to trust that you mean what you say.

In '*The Speed of Trust*,' Stephen R. Covey identifies that there are Four Cores of Credibility which make you believable to both yourself and others. All are necessary for self-trust:

Core One: Integrity

- *Walking the talk and being congruent both inside and out*
- *Courage to act in accordance with your beliefs and values*
- *Most massive violations of trust are violations of integrity*

Core Two: Intent

- *Our motives, agendas and resulting behaviour*
- *Trust grows when we genuinely care for the people we interact with, lead or serve*

Core Three: Capabilities

- *Our talents, attitudes, skills, knowledge and style that inspire confidence – they are the means we use to produce results*
- *Our ability to establish, grow, extend and restore talent*

Core Four: Results

- *Track record, performance and ability to get the right things done*
- *Credibility increases when we accomplish what we say we will do and diminishes when we fail*

The first two deal with character and the second two with competence. If we visualise these four cores of credibility as a tree, then character forms the roots of the tree, because only once that is established, can trust and then leadership follow. Importantly, your character determines your success at leadership and whether people will trust you. No one likes to spend time (i.e. follow) with people they don't trust, it simply does not make sense. Therefore a person's character communicates many things to other people:

Character Communicates Consistency

▦ *A leader needs to act consistently, day in day out, and can't decide just to quit because they are having a bad day*

Character Communicates Potential

▦ *When a leader's character is strong, people trust them and they trust in their ability to release their potential. This gives people hope for the future and boosts their personal self-esteem*

Character Communicates Respect

▦ *If you don't have character within, you cannot earn respect from others and respect is essential for lasting leadership*

How ironic it is that we spend millions of pounds annually developing competency skills in our team members when really our focus should be on developing character skills in the areas of integrity, authenticity and discipline. To develop integrity you need to become scrupulously honest, to tell the truth even when it hurts. To be authentic you need to be yourself with everyone and not play politics or pretend to be anything you are not. (Horses are master readers of authenticity as we saw in Chapter Three and can spot immediately if someone is not being authentic.)

Finally, to strengthen your discipline, you need to do the right thing regardless of how you feel. (Horses are masters at teaching discipline as, regardless of the weather, I have a commitment to go and check my horses twice a day and feed and water them – it is amazing how disciplined you can become when you know that someone or something is relying on you.)

Why we Follow Leaders...

Just like horses, people follow leaders whom they trust and feel connected to, people whose character is trustworthy. And how do they know if someone is trustworthy? Well, a large amount of this information comes from the person's body language and how they present. We have already discussed that 55% of communication is based on body language which both horses and humans can read with consummate ease.

I remember being at a Tony Robbins seminar when we were discussing body language and how it was the global currency of communication. There were over 7,000 people in the audience, all from different countries, backgrounds and walks of life and yet we could immediately connect with how each other was feeling by reading the other person's body language. For example, if someone was shy and timid their body posture would include bent-over shoulders, head down, eyesight averted, short slow steps, whereas someone who was happy and joyous would be standing tall, shoulders and head back, body open, invariably with a smile on their face. In the excellent book *The Definitive Book of Body Language – How to read others' thoughts by their gestures,* Allan and Barbara Pease reveal the myriad of different body postures and how these can be interpreted. It is a great read for anyone involved in wanting to understand better the dichotomy between what people say and what they feel.

I'm sure you have all experienced the situation when you have walked into a room and you just know instinctively that something is wrong, even though everyone is professing that things are alright. There is just something about the way the people are acting – their body language and tone of voice lets us know all is not well. Often, even when we challenge people they continue to say that everything is fine when their body language is screaming something else at us. This is a classic case of the person's words not being aligned and congruent with what they are feeling in their body. Often this occurs when people feel under pressure. The gap between what people feel and what they say is huge and can be very costly to organisations. A national survey in the US suggested that 70% of employees were afraid to speak up at work, and in other cultures this might be even higher. Imagine what might happen if only companies would muster the courage to measure the lost productivity and stress generated through unexpressed fears and concerns. I expect the results would be shocking.

Max Landsberg suggests that we seek to try to build two types of trust when seeking to lead team members:

1. *Trust in Intentions*
2. *Trust in Abilities*

Like horses, team members want to know that our intentions are honest and being open is perhaps the most powerful way that a leader can create trust. When a leader opens up, people tend to be more open in return and a genuine interest and respect can develop. Conversely, if the leader is more like a 'closed book', people find it difficult to connect with them because there is no commonality of purpose. This is the reason why open-plan offices have become more popular in recent years. The lack of closed doors makes managers and team leaders more accessible and so some of the physical barriers of communication are broken down.

Leaders are also more likely to instil trust in their team members if they demonstrate fairness, especially when making contentious decisions, and they can admit to their own Achilles' heel and seek to address this. Ultimately though, trust is developed through showing people that you are serving others (and/or a higher cause), as opposed to serving self. Building trust in your abilities is achieved through exuding appropriate optimism and confidence and ensuring that your accomplishments are recognised appropriately.

The Trust Mirror

Horses provide us with a perfect mirror of how trustworthy we are. When two horses meet for the first time, or indeed when a person meets a horse, the horse is asking three questions:

1. *Who are you?*
2. *What do you want?*
3. *How do you operate?*

Effectively the horse is seeking to assess how trustworthy you are in your intentions. Are you greeting the horse in order to make him do something for you or are your intentions simply that you want to say 'hello'? How the horse answers these questions will influence the response that you get. During that summer of 2004, when I couldn't catch my horse Toby, I suspect his answers to these questions would have been something like:

- *That is my miserable owner who only turns up at weekends.*

- *She wants to throw a saddle and bridle on me and expects me to take her for a ride.*

- *She is again being really self-serving. It is all about her, she cares nothing for my feelings or what I want from this relationship.*

Against that background it is hardly surprising that he opted to vote with his feet and not allow me to catch him. Reflecting on this situation made me think about similar questions we might unconsciously pose ourselves when we meet another person. Imagine you are going out to buy a new computer for your home. When you get to the computer store some of the questions that might run through your head as you meet the salesman for the first time are:

- *Do you care about me?*

- *Do you have the knowledge to help me?*

- *Can I trust you to make an unbiased recommendation that meets my needs and not your sales targets?*

The chances are that many of you have experienced a less than great buying experience if you could answer no to all three questions. Some of you may not have even been able to answer yes to one question. As a result, it is unlikely that you connected with, or indeed trusted the salesperson. Consequently you probably never bought the computer from that shop. I wonder what the long-term implications will be for that store where the salespeople don't care about their customers and the customers don't trust the salespeople? Maybe the answer lies in the fact that the internet is fast becoming a preferred shopping channel for many households. Rather than relying on trusting someone else, people prefer to undertake their own research and then purchase goods online. During Christmas 2011 it is estimated that some 25% of purchases were made online.

This is not to say that great salespeople don't exist; they do, and when you stumble across them they are like gold dust. My dad has an amazing relationship with Anthony, the salesman at his local Brayley Honda dealership. Anthony has been looking after my dad for some ten years now and without hesitation my dad trusts him with all the decisions he makes regarding new cars. No surprise then, that in the last decade my dad has bought five new cars there, and when unexpectedly I needed a new vehicle after mine was written off in an accident, my dad didn't hesitate in going to speak to Anthony to see how he could help. As usual he came up trumps, finding me a low-mileage second hand 4x4 that was perfect for my needs. So how did Anthony establish credibility and trust with my dad? Well, my dad changes his car every three years so, as the three year anniversary of his existing car was fast approaching, he went out to a number of local car dealerships to see what was on offer. It was just before he went on holiday so he informed the salespeople he would not be making a purchase until he got home. I remember my dad telling me that a few days after he got home he received a telephone call from Anthony asking how his holiday was and if he could be of service. Anthony was the only salesman who followed through and took action. That simple act instilled confidence in my dad that Anthony genuinely cared for him and wanted to serve him; Anthony gained credibility in my dad's eyes and in doing so earned his trust. The rest is history.

Trust Your Instincts

At the beginning of this chapter we discussed that no one will trust you unless you trust yourself. Listening to that gut instinct deep inside your body is perhaps one of the greatest gifts that you can give yourself. It is there for your self-preservation but time and time again I find myself and my clients ignoring this inner voice, preferring to listen to the rational, intellectual left brain. Being around horses teaches you never to ignore your instincts but rather to rely on them as credible, unquestionable sources of information and communication. Put simply, if we don't listen to our instincts then we can get ourselves and our equine friends into danger. Once we begin to trust our instincts then a whole new world of opportunities and possibilities opens up for us as we tune into things that we never saw before.

As prey animals, horses have to listen to and trust their instincts in order to survive. This makes them great teachers and role models for us. By contrast, over the years humans have forgotten to listen to their natural instincts. In fact many of us carry on regardless, never listening to that inner voice, or if we hear it we ignore it and then we wonder why things turn out so badly. I recall when I was working in Corporateland that I invariably failed to listen to that inner voice. I made decisions that I regretted and kept taking on new projects even though I barely had time to complete the work I already had on my desk. Quite frankly, I didn't trust my gut instinct that was telling me to slow down and stop taking on more work. The net result was that I burned out and experienced fatigue. This was the ultimate way of my body telling me to stop. I couldn't help but hear the message loud and clear when I was drained of energy. But why was it that I never listened to what was going on and blindly carried on regardless? I guess it was because I never trusted myself, I never trusted myself to listen to that inner voice with all its wisdom. I never listened to my heart and gut and the funny thing is that despite this being our instinctive reaction (our survival mechanism), society has helped us numb this feeling and so discount it from the list of rational solutions that are available. And yet, listening to our instincts isn't a sign of weakness; it is a sign of strength.

Another word for our natural instincts is our intuition. I remember a number of coaches suggesting in the past that I listen to my intuition but quite frankly I was never really sure what they meant. What was this illusive quality called intuition and indeed what did it mean? I'm ever-indebted to Liz Mitten-Ryan of Equinisity who shared with me that intuition is made up of two words: inner and tuition – so to her intuition is about listening to our inner teachings, the things that we just know about the world, our gut feeling. There is nothing to learn, we just know when something is right or wrong. Listening to these ancient teachings that have been handed down from generation to generation can help us live a more fulfilling, authentic life. I know at times in the past that I have believed I don't have any intuition but then I remember that my intuition is always working; it is just that I'm not tuned to the right radio station to hear it. If I focus and make myself open to tune in and listen to my intuition then I can hear it loud and clear – just like the radio station playing in the background in my kitchen.

Herd Dynamics - Do You Know Your Place?

*'If you want to get the best out of someone,
you must look for the best that is within them.
Leadership develops daily, not in a day.'*

John C. Maxwell

Herd Dynamics - Do You Know Your Place?

'If you want to get the best out of someone,
you must look for the best that is within them.
Leadership develops daily, not in a day.'

John C. Maxwell

There is so much we can learn from horses about teamwork and community. As prey animals horses live in herds to ensure their safety and for companionship. They have a rigid set of rules for how the group operates and this is what maintains the harmony. Every horse has their role in the herd and every horse knows their responsibilities. There is absolute clarity and, as a result, no pointless arguments or internal politics prevail. There is trust between herd members and acceptance of the hierarchy of leadership. Just compare this with society together where the cohesiveness of groups of people – whether they be teams, family units or business entities – are fuelled by fear and mistrust. No wonder then that we can learn much from horses about how to run our businesses and boardrooms more effectively.

So what is a team and why do people, like horses, instinctively want to be part of one? The reason lies in the fact that none of us want to be alone. Tony Robbins has identified what he calls the six human needs. These consist of:

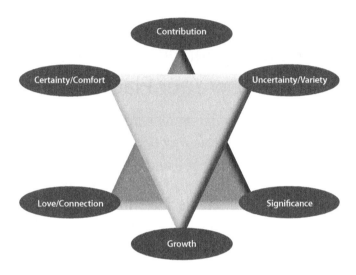

The six core values work on a type of pull-push system whereby if you get too much of one core value you then go out and seek the opposite core value.

However, before we examine this, let's just look at what the six core needs are as defined by Tony Robbins:

1. Certainty

For most people, certainty equals survival. We all need a sense of certainty that we can avoid pain and gain pleasure. Some people try to achieve certainty by trying to control everything around them. It may feel good for the moment, but it's not good for them and it's not good for those around them, nor does it serve the greater good. On the other hand, when you feel good about what you're doing, that it is good for you and you are in a courageous and faith-filled state; you tend also to do things that serve the greater good. Here's the paradox though. When a person becomes totally certain, when things are completely predictable, when you satiate this need, you become bored. So while we want certainty, we simultaneously want a certain amount of uncertainty.

2. Uncertainty/Variety

Everyone needs variety, a surprise, a challenge to feel fully alive and to experience fulfilment. With too much certainty we're bored. Likewise, with too much variety we become extremely fearful and concerned. We need a degree of certainty in our lives to experience the variety. There's a delicate balance between these two needs that must be struck for us to feel truly fulfilled. Some people choose to get variety, to feel a change in their state or the way they feel, by doing drugs or alcohol. Some people do it by watching movies. Others use stimulating conversation and opportunities to learn.

3. Significance

We all have a need for significance, a sense that we are unique in some way, that we have special purpose and meaning in our lives. Again, we try to meet this need through destructive vehicles –making ourselves unique by, for example, manufacturing a belief that we're better than everyone else. Some people become unique by developing extreme problems that set them apart from others. Medical science has now proved that some people have developed the subconscious ability to make themselves ill in order to gain the caring attention of others. Some people develop uniqueness by earning more money, having more toys, going to school and achieving more degrees or by dressing in a unique way, having a certain sense of style. Or we can choose to live a life of extraordinary service. Just remember, we all need to feel unique but, paradoxically, in order to feel unique we have to separate ourselves. If we feel totally unique we feel different and separate and this violates our need for connection and love.

4. Connection and Love

This includes feeling connected with yourself as well as with others with whom you can share your love. To meet this need, you can join a group or a club that has a positive purpose. Some individuals join a gang for negative purposes but they still achieve the feeling of connection. By aligning with your creator, and feeling like you are being guided, you can feel immediate connection. Again, some people become ill in order to feel connected and loved. Some people will steal, do drugs and drink excessive amounts of alcohol to feel a part of a group and a sense of connection. Others will perform at extraordinary levels in order to be accepted, loved or connected to a high performance team. A simple thing to remember is, as with all other human needs, if you give consistently that which you wish to receive, you tend to get it back from others.

5. Growth

Growth equals life. On this planet, everything that is alive is either growing or dying. Growth is one of the two primary needs in life. It doesn't matter how much money you have, how many people acknowledge you, what you've achieved in life; unless you feel like you're growing, you will be unhappy and unfulfilled.

6. Contribution

We all have a deep need to go beyond ourselves and to live a life that serves the greater good. It is in the moments that we do this that we experience true joy and fulfilment. Contributions are not only made to others but contributing to ourselves is a meaningful action as well, for we cannot give to others what we do not have. A balance of contribution to oneself and others, especially unselfish contribution, is the ultimate secret to the joy that so many people wish to have in their lives.

It is this need for significance and connection that drives us to want to become part of a team. As social animals we need to fit in and there is nothing more satisfying than contributing to others and feeling needed. However, if no acknowledgement is received that you are performing well and contributing to the team, then people become demotivated. People, like horses, need feedback and confirmation that they are doing a good job. Without this feedback, both people and horses become resentful and lose their sense of value. They feel like they are not needed any longer and so lose their sense of being part of the herd. I know from personal experience how this can feel.

When I worked in London I had a great job and externally I had all the trappings of success – a nice car, a lovely house and my horse – and yet invariably I felt isolated and alone. It was a tough place to be being a leader when there was very little feedback on my own performance and this is one of the reasons why many leaders burn out after years of success. They fail to gain the significance they need from the job and therefore fail to acknowledge the contribution they are making to the organisation. It is for this reason that I'm an ardent supporter of providing team members with regular feedback on their performance, focusing on the positive aspects, rather than the negative.

We are witnessing a similar situation occurring in society today. The summer riots in 2011 were, in my opinion, fuelled by a need for significance. Today, many young people feel they have nothing to offer, employment prospects are dire and in many cases the young people's self-esteem has been worn away by the number of times they have been said 'No' to. A UCLA survey from a few years ago reported that the average one-year-old child hears the word 'No' more than 400 times a day! And it is estimated that the average child hears the word 'No' or 'Don't' over 148,000 times while growing up, compared with just a few thousand 'Yes' messages. Like horses, we all crave companionship and connection with others and, for many young people, rioting and becoming part of a tribe, even just for a night, helped them feel a part of something. It fuelled their need for significance.

It is also perhaps not surprising, given the number of dysfunctional families that exist today as well as the number of people living alone, that social media has become such a powerful phenomenon in our world. Over half the UK population (around 30 million people) are believed to have a Facebook account and globally there are some 750 million registered users of Facebook. Social media provides many people with the ability to feel part of a tribe and also allows people to connect with each other in this somewhat disconnected society. Of course the irony is that the connections formed via social media sites are very shallow and many would argue whether people are really truly connected.

It's not just children that we need to be conscious of when using the word 'No'. I have two young horses that came into my care last year, as well as two older horses in my herd. The youngsters are particularly inquisitive; curious to explore, they try and get into everything, much to my frustration at times. It would be so easy to continually tell them off, but I understand how damaging that could be to their spirit and so I go out of my way to provide them with positive reinforcement for the great things they do, like standing still and leading quietly. In fact I remember once asking my equine mentor Carolyn

Resnick why she didn't do anything when a young colt she was working with started chewing his lead rope. She told me she was ignoring the behaviour, as by saying 'No' and reprimanding him she was drawing attention to what she did not want the horse to do. I'm certain this is the same within teams, as people are somehow attracted to do the very things that we don't want them to do. And if we fail to follow through and address the issue, then we lose credibility and, ultimately, trust as we discussed in a previous chapter.

The other great feature of being part of a team is that it enables us to achieve more. I just love this acronym for TEAM:

T *together*

E *everyone*

A *achieves*

M *more*

In *'The 17 Indisputable Laws of Teamwork'* John C. Maxwell asserts that *"One is too small a number to achieve greatness"'* And if you really think about it, can you recall a time in history when one act of genuine significance was achieved by just one man? On all occasions a team has been involved and so this is why President Lyndon Johnson once famously said, *"There are no problems we cannot solve together, and very few that we can solve by ourselves."*

The importance of teamwork is paramount to any organisation and all good leaders must realise that they cannot be successful without the support of team members.   Johnny Wilkinson might well have been the best rugby fly-half that England has ever seen and indeed, his spectacular drop goal in the final minute that won England the 2003 World Cup is legendary, but Johnny could not have achieved that success without the support of his teammates.   Individuals play the game, but teams win championships.   The same runs true in business: great leaders play the game but only committed, motivated employees help companies achieve great financial success.   Success is a team sport however you look at it.

Benefits of Being in a Team

There are a number of benefits of being in a team and these include:

- *Being in a team involves more people and therefore makes more resources – time, ideas and energy – available than one individual would have*

- *Teams allow a leader to maximise their potential and minimise their weaknesses*

- *Teams provide multiple perspectives on how to reach the goal as each individual will see the problem in a different light. This allows for the creative flow of ideas and stumbling blocks that one person might see can easily be navigated*

- *Teams share the credit for victories and the blame for losses. This fosters genuine humility and authentic communication*

- *Teams keep leaders accountable for the goals*

- *Teams can simply do more than the individual*

So why then do people sometimes want to do things by themselves? Some reasons might include:

- *Ego – admitting that you can't do everything. As Andrew Carnegie once declared: "It marks a big step in your development when you come to realise that other people can help you do a better job than you could do alone."*

- *Insecurity – leaders feel threatened by their team members. By failing to promote teamwork the leader undermines their own potential and erodes the best efforts of the people with whom they work. They would do well to listen to the advice of former US President Woodrow Wilson who said: "We should not only use all the brain we have, but all that we can borrow."*

- *Naiveté – underestimating the difficulty of achieving big things*

- *Temperament – some people are not very extrovert and it simply does not occur to them to think in terms of working with others. They never think to enlist the support of others; however, ironically, working alone creates huge barriers to their own potential. As Dr Allan Fromm noted: "People have been known to achieve more as a result of working with others than against them."*

However, the harsh reality is that success cannot be achieved alone. Today's current economic climate has meant that more and more people are setting up their own businesses. At the last count just over four million people in the UK were self-employed and running their own small businesses. What I witness time and time again with my clients is many of these businesses struggling to succeed. It is estimated that 80% of small businesses fail in their first year and only 20% are still in business after five years. So why is this? It is not because the business owners don't have great ideas or don't know what to do; quite simply, what I observe is many people suffering from what I call the Lone Ranger syndrome. They suffer from the isolation of working alone and with no one there to motivate, support, provide feedback and offer accountability. As we have noted, success is a team sport and even the Lone Ranger had his faithful companion, Native American Indian, Tonto, to support him on his journey.

Know Your Place in the Herd

Horses can show us how to work as a team if only we let them. As prey animals, horses have a natural desire for companionship and to be part of a herd. This is their survival mechanism because by being a Lone Ranger out on the plains there is a very high probability that they will come under attack by some predator, maybe in the shape of a mountain lion. Like a small business owner trying to keep aware and on top of all facets of the business, being alone and trying to keep yourself safe from danger 24 hours a day is a daunting task. There is no respite to sleep and rest, because if the horse stops for just one moment and loses awareness of his current environment then he might become some predator's dinner. Many small business owners that I work with feel the same – devoid of any support, they feel like they are on a never-ending rollercoaster that they can't get off, because if they do their business might fail.

Horses learn at birth the importance of the hierarchical structure of the herd. Always prepared for a potential predator, they can run within hours of being born. They instinctively know that their survival depends on listening and following the instructions of their mother and the other leaders of the herd. In moments of danger they realise that there is no time to discuss strategy: "Which way do you think we should run?" or "I think this would be the best way." These discussions are pointless as unless action is taken now they might be dead, or at least injured. Horses understand the importance of following the leader in times of crisis, and in these instances the lead mare leads from the front, setting the direction that the herd will take to escape danger. The lead mare adopts Leadership Position One that we discussed in Chapter Two.

Talent Dynamics is a great way for leaders to understand how their team members fit into the herd. Talent Dynamics is based on the ancient Chinese philosophy I Ching and it helps people and organisations get into and stay in flow (ie be aligned and congruent) based on their unique profile. We all have unique gifts – strengths – that we bring to the world and for individuals and organisations to prosper it makes sense to have people in the roles where they can utilise these strengths most effectively.

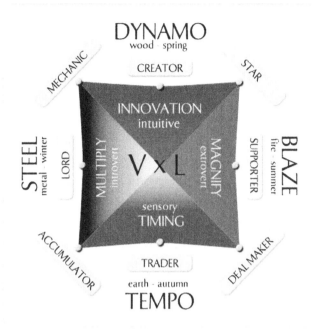

As the diagram above shows there are eight different profiles and each profile contributes to the business best in a certain way. Just imagine being a Star (who is great at marketing and improving the brand) in the role of a Lord (who is great at managing cashflow). Immediately you can see the disconnect as everyone's strengths are not being optimised. When this happens team members get disgruntled and the business gets into conflict. Trust and flow is lost as people don't feel valued in the herd as they are unable to contribute. However, align people in the best roles for them and the organisation and business flows as there is harmony and unity in the team.

Who's the Boss?

So how do horses decide who will become the leader? Well, just like people each horse has its own personality. Some horses like to be leaders – they want to take charge of the situation. Others are happy to be part of the herd and play a submissive role, just keeping a low profile and doing their thing. Others are more dominant in nature; they might profess to want the leadership role but in reality they lack the character to assume this position. What is interesting to observe is that typically when a new horse is integrated into an existing herd of horses, the new horse will allow the other horses to lead it from behind. By this I mean that the new horse allows the other horses to move him around. This act indicates to the existing herd members that the new horse is willing to be compliant and does not want to upset the hierarchy. The new horse recognises that he needs to join the herd at the bottom of the pecking order, because the desire to be included and accepted into the herd is so strong. Just like a little child going to a new school, or an employee joining a new company, our initial desire is to be accepted and to experience love and connection. We do not want to upset the apple cart on Day One and get excluded. Does that mean that the new horse will stay at the bottom of the pecking order? No, he will find ways over the upcoming days and weeks to earn his right to move up the ranks, much like employees do in new teams.

This concept was illustrated so well to me by an Arabian horse called Red Line of Fire who I looked after at the

Epona Horse Rescue in Colorado. Red had been saved from slaughter and, having spent six months rehabilitating him, it was time for him to move on to a new home. We found a lovely home for him about 20 miles away with Heidi, an experienced trainer and breeder. It was a lovely autumnal day when we delivered Red to his new home. With rolling pastures and loads of lush green grass I knew that he would be very happy there. After his abusive start in life Red was not the most sociable horse so we decided to help boost his self-confidence by letting him join a herd of six-month-old foals. Once we let him into the pasture with the new herd it was incredible to see this ten-year-old horse allowing himself to be pushed around by young foals. Red's need for acceptance far outweighed his desire to lead in that moment and so he complied. It was actually quite funny watching him acquiesce to the foals. Did he stay in this role for long? No, he soon set boundaries and claimed his position as the leader of the group, and in fact the foals were happy to allow him this role.

During the *Unbridled Success* retreats that I run I invariably get my clients to stand and observe a herd of horses and then share with me who they think is the leader of the group. At one such retreat we were running in Sweden my co-facilitator brought six horses into the arena. I had never met these horses before and it was fascinating to see what ensued and, more importantly, what the clients saw. Five of the horses engaged in high play antics, charging around the arena bucking, squealing and biting each other while one just stood back quietly and observed what was happening. Within the group there were horses of all shapes and sizes, including one very impressive large bay horse called Qurino. He had a big personality and you could not help but be awestruck by his presence – both physically and emotionally he stood out from the crowd. After twenty minutes of observing these horses we asked the clients which horse they were attracted to and why, and also who they thought was the leader of the group. It was interesting that many of the clients were drawn to the large bay horse and many people felt he was the leader because of the charisma and presence he exuded. We then asked the clients, "Imagine you are part of this herd, who would you like to negotiate your salary increase with?" That made the clients stop in their tracks and in fact no one wanted to negotiate a salary increase with the big bay horse. Why? He was intimidating and, in fact, a bully. He used his size to get what he wanted but there was little or no consideration for the other herd members. He was not a team player and therefore not the leader of the group. The actual leader of the group was a small dun-coloured horse called Scooter who just stood back quietly and observed. From this position he could clearly see everything that was happening around him and take the appropriate action when needed. He did not get involved in the herd antics but rather let the herd sort things out themselves; he trusted them and only stepped into the fray when necessary. This horse was adopting Leadership Position Three, setting the course and then letting the others get on with whatever they needed to do to make it happen.

Today, many horses are kept in domestic situations and so the natural hierarchical structure that occurs in the wild becomes interrupted. I witnessed this last year with my two horses Toby and Charlie. For about four years now Toby and Charlie have lived together, sometimes alone and sometimes as part of a larger herd – it just depends on the situation that we find ourselves in. My own preference is for my horses to be part of a large herd but that is not always possible. So on this occasion Toby and Charlie had been together for about six months when two new horses came into the yard where they were stabled. Always wanting my horses to be part of a larger group we decided to put the two new horses, Tom and Spot, in the pasture next to Toby and Charlie so they could get to know each other over the fence before integrating them. Both Toby and Charlie are quite placid horses and I felt sure that everything would be fine. I expected a bit of squealing over the fence as the horses introduced themselves to each other but not much more. Well, nothing could have prepared me for what happened that day and for many more days to come. Initially Toby and Charlie went and met Tom and Spot and all was well, but then Toby became very insecure. Worried that Charlie would no longer be his friend, he proceeded to herd him to the far side of the field and for over a week kept Charlie in a small corner of the field, far away from Tom and Spot. It was incredible the energy that Toby had to expend keeping Charlie in that small space. I was exhausted just watching it and judging by how much Toby slept when he came into his stable every night, it took a lot out of him too. Was Toby being a good leader? No, he wasn't and in my view he was actually being a bully and being very dominant with Charlie, but in the absence of another leader Toby felt it was his duty to step up to the mark and become one. The problem was that he lacked the skills and character to do it. His personality meant that he was not a natural leader. I'm sure you will be pleased to learn that since this incident Toby and Charlie are now in a larger herd with my two fillies Bracken and Thistle and my friend's horses Pilot and Tanner. The change in Toby has been profound; he is now much more comfortable, relaxed and happy as he has found his place in the herd.

Toby's predicament led me to think about companies that I have worked in and leaders I have observed and I'm convinced that, like Toby, some people are promoted to leadership roles who don't really want them. They seek to do a good job, but because the role is incongruent with their abilities they often don't succeed. However, put them in the right place in the team and give them the right role and they flourish and succeed. John C. Maxwell describes this as 'The Law of Niche'; it is the role/niche that someone has where they add most value to the team. In 2003 Johnny Wilkinson's role was that of fly-half for the English rugby team. What would have happened if Sir Clive Woodward, the then England coach, had asked Johnny to play hooker for the important World Cup Final against Australia? He would have been out of position and unable to shine and morale would have dipped in the team as they would not have been playing to their capability. The team would have become resentful, realising that they were not living up to their potential and Steve Thompson, the hooker, would have become despondent that his skills were not being utilised. The team would have lost confidence and the competition, in this case Australia, would have been well placed to benefit from the chaos that ensued. And yet too often I see this happening in companies – people placed in roles they are ill-quipped to handle and the effect on the team can be immense.

I remember this situation all too well. It was spring 2004 when I was working in London and leading a very specialised hotels and leisure team. We were in the process of recruiting some new analysts for the team and we had shortlisted a couple of candidates. Having conducted final interviews I sat with my colleague Lorna and discussed the merits of each candidate with a view to making our final decision. One of the candidates had some great skills that were lacking in the team but we were both concerned about whether they would be a good fit in both the team and the company culture. This particular individual was somewhat quirky and extrovert which was at odds with the very staid, professional culture and values of the company. The other candidate was less experienced but culturally a better fit with our team. We deliberated long and hard and, despite both of us having some concerns, we offered the job to the 'quirky' character. The candidate had only been in place a few weeks when we realised the tragic mistake we had made. We had both failed to listen to our gut instinct and now we had a major challenge. This new employee simply did not fit in; he was in the wrong position in the wrong company. The teen-style pop posters in his cubicle (the small work area each person had) were completely at odds with the other team members, and then it transpired that his work ethic was also not aligned with the company values. Yet, despite this, I insisted that we continue to mentor and develop this person and give them the benefit of the doubt – I felt I was doing the right thing. It took many months for me to see the demoralising effect that this team member was having on the others in the team. As productivity and morale within the group fell, I was forced into action for fear of the existing team members leaving. It was a humbling time - acknowledging my mistake and then taking action to rectify it. That team member was eventually counselled out of the job and harmony was restored, but it was tough lesson for me on the importance of getting the right people in the right roles.

This story clearly illustrates how having the right people in the right roles is essential to a team's success and how the dynamics of a team can change according to the placement of people:

- *Regression* – *having the wrong person in the wrong place*
- *Frustration* – *having the wrong person in the right place*
- *Confusion* – *having the right person in the wrong place*
- *Progression* – *having the right person in the right place*
- *Multiplication* – *having the right people in the right places*

It does not matter what kind of team or herd you are dealing with; the principles are the same. All players have a place where they add the most value and when each person does the job that is best for them, everybody wins. David Ogilvy summed this up well when he said, *"A well-run restaurant is like a winning baseball team. It makes the most of every crew member's talent and takes advantage of every split-second opportunity to speed up service."*

The other thing that I learned from this experience is that attitude is catching. I had never realised before what a damning effect the bad attitude of one team member could have on the entire team. It is what John C. Maxwell calls *'The Law of the Bad Apple'.* Whilst it is true that a good attitude among team members does not guarantee success, a bad attitude guarantees its failure and, if left alone and unaddressed, that bad attitude will cause dissension, resentment, combativeness and division within the team. Like a rotten apple in a basket of fresh green apples it will eventually infect all the good apples, turning them rotten. It is therefore imperative that a leader addresses the bad attitude at the earliest opportunity or else the effect, as I found out, can be damaging beyond belief.

Horses understand the importance of having a good attitude to maintain harmony in the herd. What you will observe is that if a horse gets out of line and fails to abide by the rules, they are chased out of the herd. The bad apple is ejected. The leader acts decisively to make this happen and the offending horse is kept on the fringes of the herd until it is repentant and invited back into the fold. If we recall that the one thing that a horse hates more than anything is being alone – it is simply not safe – then this punishment is very fitting. Once the 'bad' horse has realised the error of his ways he is invited back into the herd and, rest assured, he will return with a much improved attitude.

Perhaps the most decisive act of removing a bad apple or weak link from the herd I have ever seen was in a documentary by Ginger Kathrens that followed Cloud, a wild stallion, and his herd in the Rocky Mountains of Montana. As I recall, it was spring and a number of the mares in the herd were giving birth to new foals. It transpired that one particular foal was born with some defects and he was unable to get up and join the herd. The inability of the young foal to move with the herd potentially put the entire herd at risk of attack from predators, so the stallion, the male leader of the group, killed the foal. As harrowing as it was to watch this scene it reminded me of how sometimes leaders have to make tough decisions for the good of the team.

How many leaders is enough in a team

Typically in the wild a herd of horses is led by two leaders: the lead mare, who positions herself at the front of the herd, and her counterpart, the resident stallion, who positions himself at the rear. The lead mare and stallion work in tandem to keep the herd organised and safe; one does not lead over the other but rather they co-ordinate within their respective roles. The stallion's main role is that of protector, keeping the herd safe from impending danger, whilst the role of the lead mare is to set the direction and decide what to do, where to go and how quickly to move. When chaos erupts the stallion refers to the lead mare in setting the direction of travel, and assumes the role of sweeper, pushing the entire herd forward. The stallion also keeps the younger horses in check and trains future stallions in the physical prowess they will need to defend their own herds.

What is often overlooked is that the lead mare and stallion rely on some important lieutenants to ensure their success. Often it is one of the other mares that senses danger first and then communicates that to the lead mare who decides what to do. These lieutenants provide the lead mare with feedback on what is happening in the ever-changing environment. They also assist her in the day-to-day running of the herd, making sure that the younger horses are taught acceptable behaviour. Some of the mares, however, prefer to stay on the edge of the herd, looking out for predators – but whatever their position, each horse knows what their role is and how it contributes to the success of the herd. So as we have seen previously, the herd survives and prospers because everyone knows their position. The herd's success rests on this premise just as the success of any team rests on each team member understanding how they contribute to the overall success of the team.

In her book *Horse Sense for the Leader Within,* Arianna Strozzi states: *"Hierarchies exist throughout the animal kingdom in order to support survivability of the species as a whole. It is a basic requirement for effective co-ordination."* Whilst we can clearly identify the hierarchies that exist within horse herds, human hierarchies are often more difficult to discern. Perhaps one of the reasons for this is that in the human world we often assume that in a hierarchy only one person has the power. I believe that this is a false presumption to make as in reality, a good leader cannot be successful without the support of others, just like the lead mare needs the support of her lieutenants. Perhaps the main difference, however, lies in the fact that within a horse herd leadership is never a given. The lead mare's and stallion's positions are continually reassessed by the other herd members and if they fail to meet up, they are challenged. The fact that the leadership positions are continually under threat ensures that the lead mare and stallion never get rusty, but continually seek to develop better leadership skills. The feedback from other herd members helps keep them operating at their optimum level and ensures that they don't become lazy or complacent and thus miss something significant that could put the entire herd in jeopardy. I wonder what would happen to companies if the leaders knew that their position was always being evaluated and that they could be usurped at any moment? Would it have stopped the fat cat crisis and financial meltdown that we have just experienced?

In Chapter Four we discussed how communication was essential to the lifeblood of any organisation and therefore it follows that if there is good communication between team members then productivity will increase and people will feel more valued and motivated. They will become more connected to the organisation they are working for. Communication creates interaction and it is this interaction that creates results. Perhaps the most extreme example of how communication can turn around an organisation was demonstrated by Gordon Bethume who changed the fortunes of Continental Airlines. When

Bethume joined the company in 1994 it was a mess; it had gone through bankruptcy twice and had ten leaders in as many years. The company had not made a profit in a decade and flight schedules were erratic. It was reported that the company had three times as many complaints as any other airline. There was massive distrust within the company and a massive lack of co-operation between teams. Bethume set about changing the culture of the organisation and whilst this did not happen overnight, his policy of engaging with team members and sharing his plans for the company's turnaround and his accessibility to employees to answer any questions they had, contributed massively to getting people back on track. Employees begun to trust their leader for the first time in decades and as a result the company turned round from posting a loss of US$204 million in 1994 to generating a profit of US$202 million in 1995.

What Bethume's approach clearly demonstrates is that team success is dependent on the quality of leadership. Would General Electric (GE) have gained the respect of the corporate world without Jack Welch? Would the US have sealed victory in the Gulf War without the leadership of Generals Norman Schwarzkopf and Colin Powell? Whatever team you are part of, its success is dependent on the leadership. So whether you are leading a company of thousands of employees, or a team of just ten people, or even seeking to be a leader for your horse or your own life, the outcome of that relationship will be due in large part to your leadership capability.

Have You Built Strong Fences?

*'Leadership is based on inspiration,
not domination, on co-operation,
not intimidation.'*

William Arthur Wood

Have You Built Strong Fences?

*'Leadership is based on inspiration,
not domination, on co-operation, not intimidation.'*
William Arthur Wood

Have you ever felt abused and violated in a relationship? Have you ever experienced a relationship going stale and uncomfortable and you just don't know why? Well, you are not alone and yet many people fail to see this coming. We enter into relationships – whether business or personal – just assuming that everything will work out fine and when it doesn't we become angry and frustrated. So what is going on that causes this situation?

The relationship with my young filly Bracken illustrates this perfectly. You might recall that Bracken came to me having been abandoned and was quite fearful of people. So during the early months with me I was very lenient with her. I accepted all types of behaviour from her that I probably would not accept with my other horses because I was so glad that she wanted to engage with me. I wanted her to be curious and come up to me and in doing so, I thought I would earn her trust. As the months passed,

Bracken and I became inseparable as our connection deepened. Every time I drove into the yard where the horses are stabled she would whinny to me across the field and then trot up to the gate to say 'good morning.' I felt on top of the world; this pony loved me so much and wanted to be with me, it was an amazing feeling. Slowly, slowly I realised however that Bracken was taking over the leadership role. She started pushing her shoulder into me when I was leading her and barging out of her stable when I fed her. I was mortified that this lovely pony was turning into a monster – and as she was growing rapidly in size, I was soon going to have some real problems. As I took a step back to review what was happening I had another AHA! moment: Bracken no longer respected me. I'm sure you have all heard of the saying *'familiarity breeds contempt'* and that was what had happened in my relationship with Bracken. She had violated my boundaries and because I had done nothing to redress the situation she had assumed her behaviour was fine and she could carry on as she wished. My inaction had caused her to lose any respect for me and, as any experienced horse person will tell you, working with a horse that does not respect your personal space is a dangerous place to be.

Over the following months I worked hard to re-earn my trust and respect with Bracken and it is one of the most tiring and energy-draining activities I have ever had to do. You see, Bracken no longer believed that I was serious when I asked her to move out of my personal space because I had set up a dynamic that meant that in the past I had not followed through. I had lost credibility with her. I now had to muster all my inner-strength to show her that I was now serious and 'move' meant 'move now'. I had to reset boundaries with her and show her that I was serious about them. Together, Bracken and I have worked things out and now we are equally respectful of each other's personal space, because let's face it, if I need my personal space then surely she has a right to hers too.

Whilst feeling humiliated that I managed to get myself into this situation with Bracken, it has been one of the best learning experiences that I could ever have as it has shown me the value and importance of setting clear boundaries in relationships. For many of the women clients I work with, setting boundaries is a real challenge. Like me, many are unaware that they are letting their spouse, partner, colleagues – or even horse – run all over them. They are oblivious to the fact that their partner no longer respects them and yet by not setting boundaries they are setting themselves up potentially for all sorts of abuse.

In her book *Brilliance Unbridled*, Kendall Summerhawk likens personal boundaries to fences – an analogy that resonates strongly with me. My horses trust the boundary that the fencing at my barn gives them as it keeps them safe and secure and, incredibly, the fencing does not need to be that strong to keep them in. They respect it and rarely try to escape – except, on occasions, Bracken! However, should I ever fail to pay attention to the fence line and it fell down, then I would lose control over my herd and they could escape. Personal boundaries are just like fences – we need to maintain them in order to keep ourselves safe.

So what are personal boundaries and how do we set and maintain them?

The purpose of having boundaries is to protect and take care of ourselves. We need to be able to tell other people when they are acting in ways that are not acceptable to us. A first step is starting to know that we have a right to protect and defend ourselves, that we have not only the right but the duty to take responsibility for how we allow others to treat us. Personal boundaries help us enjoy healthy relationships and attract people into our life who are positive forces and build our self-worth. Personal boundaries factor into creating a rich, fulfilling life that keeps us in control of our destiny.

1. Saying No
– Personal boundaries are defined in part by knowing when to say 'No' and not feeling guilty about it. You are not expected to do everything anyone asks of you.

2. Values
– Healthy personal boundaries are based on your own moral beliefs. Going against your values for another person means that you may want to reassess your relationship with them.

3. Identity
– Personal boundaries can help you form your identity because they force you to evaluate what you want and what you don't want in your life, and enforce those guidelines.

4. Speak Up
– When others cross your personal boundaries, tell them. You don't have to fight with them to let them know where you stand, but calmly talking about your boundaries enforces your sense of self and purpose.

5. Trust
– Above all, don't let others tell you that your personal boundaries are unacceptable. They do not live in your skin. You know what you need better than anyone else.

Setting boundaries is not a more sophisticated way of manipulation, although some people will say they are setting boundaries when in fact they are attempting to manipulate. The difference between setting a boundary in a healthy way and manipulating is when we set a boundary we let go of the outcome. For this reason, it is impossible to have a healthy relationship with someone who has no boundaries, with someone who cannot communicate directly and honestly. Learning how to set boundaries is a necessary step in learning to be a friend to ourselves. It is our responsibility to take care of ourselves, to protect ourselves when it is necessary. It is impossible to learn to be loving to ourselves without owning our self and owning our rights and responsibilities as co-creators of our lives.

So how we interact with a horse can teach us a lot about the personal boundaries in our own lives. A young lady, we shall call her Emma, came to me for some Horse Assisted Coaching wanting to work on boundaries. As I chatted with her before the session started, she shared a number of examples of when she had failed to set boundaries in her own life. Reflecting on her childhood she realised that from a really early age she had never learned to set boundaries. She always felt, as many women do, that if she set boundaries then no one would like her. She always wanted to make her parents proud of her and so she agreed to do whatever she was asked, never saying 'No' to anyone. In her teenage years this inability to say 'No' got her into real trouble as she began to date young men, and in the end, resulted in her falling pregnant. This pattern of behaviour continued when she started work. Her strong work ethic meant that she rapidly became a star employee for the company she worked for but her inability to set boundaries and say 'No' meant that her boss just gave her more and more work. Soon she found herself in a position of feeling overwhelmed and burned-out. She simply couldn't cope any longer. The fact that her fence had always been broken meant that her boss took advantage of her good nature and in the end Emma's health suffered. Of course the irony of the situation was that Emma felt that by being compliant and accepting and delivering all the work her boss gave her, she would be liked more. However, what actually happened was that her boss lost all respect for her. She became like a doormat that he could walk all over and gradually the relationship between the two of them broke down. In my experience, in relationships people actually like feedback and someone 'pushing back' at them. There is nothing to engage with if the other person is always agreeable and so the relationship loses energy and sparkle.

Given her experiences it was no wonder that Emma was somewhat apprehensive as she stepped out into the round pen to work with a small black pony named Thistle. I gave Emma a reed, which is a piece of willow about five foot long, and told her all I wanted her to do was stand in the round pen with Thistle and if Thistle approached her she was to use the reed to keep the pony away. Being a very friendly pony, Thistle started approaching and at first, Emma just let her. Almost as if frozen in fear, she stood there doing nothing to protect her boundaries. Thistle walked assertively up to Emma, nuzzled her and then went away. As Emma and I discussed what had just happened she shared with me that she was afraid that the pony might not like her. I argued that in my experience, Thistle valued great leadership and she just wanted Emma to be clear about what was acceptable. "She needs you to step up and be a leader and assert your power over your personal space," I told her.

The next time Thistle started to approach Emma, she succeeded in keeping the pony out of her personal space by swishing the reed in front of her and stating that her intent was for Thistle to stay out of her personal space. Interestingly, after this interaction, Thistle's demeanour changed. She became more interested and curious towards Emma, seeking to find a way to interact and connect with her. Thistle continued to try to violate Emma's personal boundaries by approaching her, and every time Emma succeeded in keeping the pony away until eventually, Thistle quit and went to explore another part of the round pen. The relief on Emma's face was clearly visible now that she had earned respect from Thistle, who knew that if Emma said 'No' she meant 'No'. After about five minutes Thistle started to approach Emma again, gingerly. I asked

Emma how she felt about the pony approaching and she said she wanted her to approach, so I suggested that she let Thistle approach and stand about three feet away from her. Emma let Thistle approach and then, when she was three feet away, she asked her to stop and the pony stopped immediately. Once again you could see the relief on Emma's face as she managed to achieve this task. After a few minutes I suggested that Emma go up and stroke Thistle but, as she approached, Thistle turned around and walked away. At first Emma was really upset by this but, as we reviewed what had happened, it became clear to her that if she wanted Thistle to respect her personal space, then she needed to respect Thistle's personal space. Relationships are always a two-way dialogue and each party must be aware of the other's needs; however this can only happen if both parties communicate their respective requirements. The other important lesson that Emma learned that day was that boundaries are flexible. Sometimes it is acceptable to let a horse into your personal space and sometimes it is not; it just depends. Also Emma began to understand how everyone is happier and clearer when they know where each other's boundaries lie. It means that everyone knows the rules of the game and has a blueprint for interacting with you.

During my time working in the corporate world I witnessed time and time again the effect that not setting clear boundaries had – both on relationships and also on the performance of the business. I witnessed people taking on responsibilities that they simply did not have the capability to discharge, and the effect was that not only did that person lose respect with their peers, they compromised their own integrity and, ultimately, control over their own life. They failed to be leaders of their own lives. Lack of focus, productivity and feelings of being overwhelmed, just as Emma experienced, combined with self-doubt and low self-esteem, are all signs that we have broken boundaries (our fences are down). Yet the good news is that it only needs some slight action to start repairing the broken boundaries and we can feel revitalised and energised.

Leadership is a Relationship

Developing boundaries and engendering respect are key components of building successful relationships. But what constitutes a relationship? Merriam-Webster's dictionary lists several definitions for the word relationship. The term is generally used to denote family ties, but it's also used as a state of connecting or binding participants. Actions that bring people together and bind them in a common cause are the key to building effective relationships. From this it follows that a leader's role encompasses that of building relationships.

In their book *The Leadership Challenge*, James Kouzes and Barry Posner state that *"Leadership is a relationship"* and explain in great detail the importance of building camaraderie among the people you are leading. When you have a meaningful relationship with another person you work more effectively together. You have a common goal and a consistent purpose. Your efforts are channelled towards the same outcome.

Effective leaders recognise the importance of building solid relationships. They spend time focusing their efforts in key areas that will build connections with the people they lead. Here are three simple tools that great leaders use to improve their working relationships:

- **Listen:** *Leaders let other people talk and they pay attention to what they're saying. They remove anything that would distract from their conversations and focus on what people are trying to convey*

- **Understand:** *They appreciate what other people do and value their contributions. Leaders are not only open to new ideas but are also eager to learn new things. They know that taking the time to understand where people are coming from will pay dividends in the long run*

- **Acknowledge:** *Leaders acknowledge the contributions of others. They are quick to give credit to others for their successes. They celebrate achievements and delight in the accomplishments of their team. They know that people will be more motivated to work hard and try new things if their leader acknowledges their efforts*

These three traits are very readily recognised in the dynamics of any herd. The horses always pay attention to each other and spend time acknowledging each other's presence by simply being companionable. The herd members also implicitly understand the contribution that the lead horses and their lieutenants make to the success of the herd. When working with and being a leader for my horses, I too have to exhibit these characteristics. I always need to be aware of how my horse is feeling by being in the moment and not distracted by mundane thoughts. I also know that my horse will perform better if he receives regular positive feedback on how he is doing, and I always acknowledge when my horse tries anything I ask. It is this continual positive feedback loop that helps boost my horse's self-esteem and keeps him wanting to deliver more. My corporate experience was just the same. Fail to build relationships and acknowledge and appreciate team members and you will never gain their commitment to help build a successful business.

Peter Drucker summed up so well why leaders need to pay attention to relationships and acknowledge and respect each other when he said:

> *"Manners are the lubricating oil of an organisation. It is a law of nature that two moving bodies in contact with each other create friction. This is as true for human beings as it is for inanimate objects. Manners – simple things like saying 'please' and 'thank you' and knowing a person's name or asking after her family – enable two people to work together whether they like each other or not. Bright people, especially bright young people, often do not understand this. If analysis shows that someone's brilliant work fails again and again as soon as co-operation from others is required, it probably indicates a lack of courtesy – that is, a lack of manners."*

All too often in the corporate world we become stuck in the busyness of the situation and forget to engage and build relationships with other people – and, in my view, these should not just be peer relationships. A good leader builds relationships across the organisation. Perhaps because my initial training was in the hospitality industry I have a strong service ethic and really appreciate the value of all team members to helping my success. Yet when I worked in Corporateland I often observed managers not engaging with support staff. I'll never forget one day going to pick up some printing from our internal printers. This is something I did regularly as to me it seemed to make sense to get to know the people who could help me get my client reports and publications out on time. During the course of one conversation the guys in the print room suddenly became aware of the fact that I was a director in the firm. You should have seen the look of horror on their faces; they simply could not believe a director was picking up their own printing. Some may argue that it was not the best use of my time but rest assured, the guys in the print room always went beyond the call of duty helping get me and my team out of sticky situations when we were running late with deadlines. To me, investing in developing those relationships paid back time and time again as I always managed to get their assistance when everyone else was being told that the deadline was not achievable.

Women, Leadership and Relationships

Today, although the number of successful women in senior positions in business is increasing, it is still a small minority. In 2011, only twelve of the Fortune 500 companies were run by women, yet women are gaining prevalence in more senior business positions. So what traits do these women have that make them successful? In her book *Horse Sense for the Leader Within,* Arianna Strozzi states:

> *"Over 70% of the powerful executives I have met or worked with rode horses as teenagers. Over 30% of them continue to ride in spite of their busy lives.*
> *I believe it is because they learned from the horse how to be assertive, confident, declarative and passionate and they translated these qualities into the other areas of their lives naturally and without thought. Most don't relate their present leadership abilities to their earlier years of practising horsemanship. They take for granted that moving a thousand pounds of living mass is not as easy as it looks on the surface, and neither is human leadership."*

What these women have come to understand is that establishing leadership and authority requires trust and respect, and not dominance created through fear and intimidation. They are very clear on what is acceptable and what is not. They know when to say 'No' and mean it. For horses, trust and respect are the cornerstones of any relationship. This does not mean that we can be wishy-washy but rather we need to show the horses clear, directive and assertive leadership, just like in the boardroom. Once a horse sees and experiences our assertive leadership and knows that we are serious in our intent then they will relax, lick and chew and follow us anywhere. By establishing leadership the horse understands his position in the herd hierarchy and then relinquishes the desire to challenge this until such time as the leader fails to maintain the role.

It's All About Energy

*'Your first and foremost job as a leader
is to take charge of your own energy
and then help to orchestrate the energy
of those around you.'*

Peter Drucker

It's All About Energy

'Your first and foremost job as a leader is to take charge of your own energy and then help to orchestrate the energy of those around you.'

Peter Drucker

I don't know whether you liked physics at school or not. I know I didn't really like the theory but I loved the practical sessions, trying out and exploring new concepts, especially trying to understand more about energy. So what is energy and what can horses teach us about it? Scientists have shown us through quantum physics that everything in the universe is made up of energy and the form that the object takes depends on the vibration of the energy. It therefore stands to reason that humans are made up of pure energy.

From a spiritual viewpoint we are deathless souls within a physical body, a particle of the Divine, of the Creator, The Source – God. In his book *A Happy Pocket Full of Money,* David Cameron says:

"Science shows us that everything is made up of energy and exchanges that with everything else at all times in a most complex way. It is the building block of all matter. The same energy that composes your flesh is the same one that composes the bricks of your house and the trees outside. It is all the same. It is constantly at flow, changing form all the time. This is a very simple explanation of a rather complex thing."

The other interesting fact about energy is that it cannot be created or destroyed – the law of conservation – but rather energy mutates into different forms. If you think about water it is comprised of two hydrogen and one oxygen molecule (H_2O) and yet water can exist in many different states. When the temperature drops below 0°C or 32°F water freezes and becomes ice, whereas when the temperature rises and exceeds 100°C or 212°F, water converts to steam. What is happening at these different temperatures is that the water molecules are vibrating at different speeds and so creating very different outcomes. The less vibration between molecules, the more solid the substance appears.

For many of my clients, particularly those from the corporate world, when I start to talk about the importance of energy their eyes glaze over and they look at me aghast. I confess that I was one of those people until about five years ago when I was introduced to the concept of the Law of Attraction by one of my mentors, John Assaraf. So please humour me while I share this important concept with you. If you subscribe to the fact that everything is energy it stands to reason that everything in the world has a vibration point at which it resonates. Now the Law of Attraction states that 'like attracts like' which means that one vibration attracts a similar vibration to it, so if all of our bodies are energy and everything around us is energy then it stands to reason that we are then connected with each other and to everything around us. If this is the case, we are entangled and everything we do – how we behave and how we think and feel – will be vibrating into this field or sea of energy. Hence it is affecting everyone in it – either directly or indirectly. I found this a very scary concept when I first heard about it but it makes perfect sense.

The Heart's Electromagnetic Field

Research has shown that the heart has an electromagnetic field which can be measured up to ten feet away from the body using current technology. Therefore, the heart's electromagnetic field envelops not only every cell in our body but also extends in all directions into the space around us. Furthermore, research conducted by the Institute of HeartMath suggests that the heart's field is an important carrier of information. This is why we can sense how someone else is feeling, even though we may not be touching them. There is also a marked difference in the frequency of the vibration that the electromagnetic field has depending on our emotional state. If we are frustrated and emotionally negative, then the frequency is noisy and disjointed, representing an incoherent state. However, when we are in a positive emotional state, for example, feeling appreciation and gratitude, then the frequency of the electromagnetic waves is clear, ordered and harmonious. This is why it is so important when giving team members appreciative feedback for a job well-done that you mean it, because believe me they will know when you don't, as your emotional vibrations will be incongruent. However, unlike horses, your team members are less likely to draw attention to this fact.

Bob Proctor, a famous philosopher and advocate of the Law of Attraction describes a feeling as *"The conscious acknowledgement of the type of vibration we are in".* Therefore, if we say that we are not feeling well, then what we are really saying is that we are in a negative vibration. Any emotion we therefore experience is just 'energy in motion'. Furthermore, it follows that if we are in a negative vibration then we will attract other negative experiences to us, since like attracts like. This is why many coaches encourage us to have a positive attitude and indeed, if you look at successful people today, they have a very positive outlook on life and are happy with where they are. Our vibrating, positive energy can influence those around us just as our negative energy can. The good news is that we control the vibration we emit. We can either choose to be happy (positive) or choose to be sad (negative). We simply need to direct our mind and lead it to the vibration we want to be in, rather than letting our mindset make the decision for us.

Horses as Energy Barometers

Being a prey animal, horses have extraordinary acuity of awareness as it is important for them to know how the other horses in the herd are feeling – are they anxious or relaxed? The energy of the other herd members will signal to a horse how to respond. Horses therefore use emotion as information to help them stay safe. They can sense the slightest shift in breathing, or muscles tightening of one of the herd members, and often these signals are imperceptible to the human eye. This is why horses prove to be such great energy barometers as they can help us understand how we feel often before we even know how we feel! If I was in any doubt, I now know by the response that I get from my horses when I go to the barn how they feel I'm feeling. Often it is easy to delude ourselves that everything is all right – our rational brain is very good at that – when in fact our body is crying out something else.

Linda Kohanov in *'The Message Behind the Emotions'* refers to emotion as being 'the sixth sense' for the reason that *"Its organ is the entire body, not a specific orifice. This sense does not function at the skin-level of touch, but as an internal excitation brought about by resonance – much like sympathetic strings resonate to an outside sound even though they have not been struck or bowed directly."* So where do emotions come from? Recent work by Candance Pert, PhD. and other researchers active in the field of psychoneuroimmunology has revealed that the molecules which carry emotional intelligence (called neuropeptides) are not only generated in the brain, but by sites throughout the body, most dramatically in the heart and the gut. This is why when people say that have a 'gut feeling' they are not speaking metaphorically, and why it is important that we listen to these instinctive feelings that we all have. Horses have some 100 feet of gut which is why they are able to tune into our emotions and energy so well. Aligned to this, horses, like other animals, also have an ability to read our intentions. I know when I was in Africa I was always amazed how on occasions the zebras and wildebeest would seem unconcerned as a lion, who had just eaten a large meal after a kill, would walk right through the area where they were grazing. However, the zebras and wildebeest would instinctively know when that same lion was looking for supper and scatter appropriately if he revealed his presence.

It is this same sensitivity to emotional energy and the intention behind it that enables horses to help reveal when we are being incongruent and putting on a happy mask when our entire being is shouting out something else. The body language of someone pretending to be happy is typically misaligned with the rise in blood pressure, muscle tension and emotional energy transmitted unconsciously by someone who is actually afraid, frustrated or angry. It is this incongruence that troubles horses and results in them mirroring the precise emotion that is being suppressed. Once the person consciously acknowledges the feelings they are experiencing and removes the mask then the horse will invariably sigh, lick their lips or show some other visible sign of relief.

During the *Unbridled Success* retreats we often have people who come along who are afraid of horses. Whilst in itself this is not a problem to us, it can become a problem for the horses, especially if the participants fail to acknowledge that fear. Because what is fear? Merely:

F *False*

E *Expectations*

A *Appearing*

R *Real*

I notice that the problem is compounded if just one person in the group is afraid, or indeed if that person is the leader of the team. They foolishly believe that they can't show this fear in front of their colleagues and so they put on a mask of bravery, whereas they are in fact quaking in their boots.

My horses immediately pick up on this and I can immediately tell from their antics what is happening. Just getting the person to acknowledge to themselves that they are afraid immediately calms the situation, and yet on some occasions, some of my clients can't even do this. Wearing the mask has become too ingrained for them to let it go. Horses therefore make split-second adjustments to both positive and negative changes in a person's behaviour and emotional state, offering constant feedback and thus timely rewards or consequences for the person's actions and feelings.

Focused Energy

As discussed earlier, to be a good communicator and connector with people requires energy but not just any old type of energy. The energy must match the situation.

Generally speaking, people will be attracted to people with higher energy as they come across as energetic, exciting and interesting. Often there is something almost contagious about their energy. However, the energy needs to be focused and directed or else ironically, it can becoming draining. I have a friend who is really high energy and most of the time is a delight to be around; however, on occasions her energy is so unfocused it just goes everywhere. It is like a box of fireworks exploding in front of you and you just don't know where to focus. This disparate energy actually leaves me feeling exhausted having been in her presence rather than energised.

As a leader it is important that your energy is directed and focused in order to get the best results from your team members. The diagram opposite shows the different levels of energy and focus and the outcomes of each combination:

- **Hesitant Leader** – *low energy and low focus*
  Blames circumstances and allows other people to dominate. Often plays the victim role

- **Occupied Leader** – *high energy and low focus*
  Feels people confused as to what they want

- **Distanced Leader** – *low energy and high focus*
  People work for the leader

- **Effective Leader** – *high energy and high focus*
  These leaders are in flow with their teams working with them. Everyone has clarity and momentum

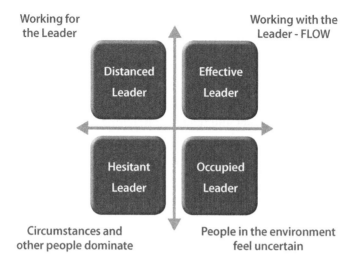

Working for the Leader

Working with the Leader - FLOW

Distanced Leader

Effective Leader

Hesitant Leader

Occupied Leader

Circumstances and other people dominate

People in the environment feel uncertain

Just like people, horses prefer people to have focused, directed energy. This is simply more appealing to be around and encouragingly reassuring. I remember one day when I was a participant in a Horse Assisted Coaching workshop, as part of my training I was asked to choose a horse and lead it through a series of obstacles including bending poles. My first dilemma was which horse to select. I had a choice of working with Bo, my firm favourite, or Prudence, a mare that I did not connect with at all. I remember thinking it would be more fun to do it with Bo and, given our great relationship, I knew the exercise would be easy and so not much of a challenge or learning experience. Well, that's what I thought at least. My rational brain of course was telling me to work with Prudence as that would take me out of my comfort zone. Eventually, after much deliberation, it was decided that I could work with both horses. So off I went with Bo to start the obstacle course.

To begin with he was a star, doing everything perfectly and as I was getting bored, I decided to up the ante. I began to run and sing whilst leading him and generally play the fool. My energy was high but really unfocused as I had no clear plan. Bo began to get annoyed and lightly grabbed my jacket and tugged at it, telling me to refocus, but I just ignored him. Bo and I weaved back through the bending poles with me still prancing around and not being very present until such point that Bo bit me really hard on my arm. Now Bo never bites so I knew I must have really upset him and, quite frankly, I was really angry and upset at him for biting me. I felt quite affronted by his actions. I dropped the rope and walked away to refocus and reflect on what had just transpired. I'll never forget the poignancy of the lessons I learnt that day which included:

- *The need to stay focused and keep my energy directive*
- *Learning is available at all times if we will just listen for it*
- *Events do not have to be complicated. There is much learning in the simplest tasks*

If you do not believe that horses can feel energy and read our body language then you only have to watch someone in a round pen with a horse. The trainer standing in the middle of the round pen can influence the speed at which the horse moves by simply altering their physiology. If the trainer drops their energy lower into his abdomen and breathes out, the horse will slow down whereas if the trainer raises their energy the horse will speed up. If

I want my horse to slow down I inhale slowly and think of my lungs and lower abdomen filling up like a balloon. The more air that I can get into the balloon the heavier it will become and the more grounded I will feel. This highlights the importance that our state can have on those around us.

Why our Energy Vibration is Important to Business

Donna Eden, the woman behind energy medicine, reveals how our energy vibration impacts others. She has some great videos on YouTube showing this but in essence what she shows is that if your energy is low, or alternatively very scrambled, then people cannot comprehend the message you are sending. Donna demonstrates this by getting someone to come on stage and read from a book. As the gentleman reads from the book she tests his energy which is weak, scrambled and unfocused. Correspondingly, the delegates in the audience, who have previously indicated high energy and focus levels, also test weak for their energy levels. However when the participant reads from the book backwards (i.e. from right to left) his energy levels become higher and more focused and interestingly, the audience all report higher levels of energy. This is important because what it clearly shows is that our energy levels impact our level of communication with others. If our energy is low then people will not receive and understand our message and vice versa. So why is this? The reason lies in the fact that our physical body copies our energy body. So if our energy body is weak, overwhelmed and can't focus, our physical body adopts these same traits. The audience subconsciously reads our body language and disconnects and so does not understand the communication that is being delivered. Just think about the implications this has in business. If your energy is low and disconnected then you put out scrambled energy, which helps explain why sometimes people cannot connect with you. Reflecting on my own experiences, it is interesting now to realise that on the days I felt like I was running on empty I was least effective at work, since my team members did not understand what I was telling them. How often in corporate life do we feel drained and then wonder why our day does not turn out to be as successful as we had hoped?

As a coach and trainer I am well aware of the energy it takes to connect with others. The capability to connect, just like in radio and TV sets, is to be able to adapt and to operate in several wavelengths, reaching the ones on which most of your audience operate. When I was a kid, I used to play 'join the dots'. If you did not join them properly your picture would not come out right. We need to learn to 'join the dots' in order to connect with people. We are all different, yet in many ways we are all the same. We all want to be successful, we all want to be loved, we all want to live a good life – so if we can connect with each other, although we are different, we can maximise each other's potential. When you learn what makes a person 'tick', you can then understand their motives, their ideals, their goals. I've heard people say "No one understands me." So many times we write those types of people off when in reality we should connect with them and get a better perspective of where they are coming from; it will help you to help them get where they need to go. Why don't you connect with someone today? Maybe a work colleague who is very different from you or someone who doesn't fit your mould. Take the energy to connect and understand them by reaching them on their wavelength and you just might be surprised at what you find.

State of Being – Physiology Affects State

If our bodies are composed of energy it follows that our physiology and emotions are by-products of how our energy is moving in our bodies. Emotions are often described as being Energy in Motion and the resonance of that energy will impact the emotion that we are feeling. We have all heard the saying that someone is 'in the zone'. Typically, we use this phrase to refer to high performance athletes who get themselves into such a state of focus and concentration that nothing can distract them from the task at hand. Their energy is laser-like and every cell of their body is committed to the task they are about to undertake. A great example of this is Linford Christie. If you watch a video of him preparing for the 100 metres final at the 1992 Olympic Games in Barcelona, where he subsequently won a gold medal, you can visibly see the focus and commitment every part of his being has towards winning. His physiology is that of a winner and he believes that he can win. He is in a winning state and that is infectious; not only does it impact his entire being, but it also impacts those around him. His motivation to succeed comes from the burning desire to achieve a purpose, to be Olympic champion.

In 1937 Napoleon Hill was commissioned by Andrew Carnegie, an industrialist and philanthropist and incidentally, one of the most powerful men in the world, to interview more than 500 wealthy and successful people in order to determine their simple formula for success. After twenty years of exhaustive research, Hill published the '*Law of Success*' that was distilled nine years later into '*Think and Grow Rich*.' One of Hill's findings was that

> "*Whatever the mind of man can conceive and believe the mind can achieve.*"

The important part here is not only that the mind can conceive what is going to happen but the mind also believes it will happen. Linford Christie was certain of his success and so gained the recognition and rewards he deserved for his hard work. Contrast this with the experience of Andre Agassi. In 1990 Agassi was at the top of his game; however, in the final of the US Open his confidence disappeared and he lost the final to Pete Sampras, someone whom he had beaten easily the previous year. Over the following few years Agassi struggled to get his performance back on track, until one day someone suggested that he review some videos of his recent games as well as some videos of his earlier years. The answer was staring him in the face. It was not that Agassi's technical game had deteriorated dramatically but rather his belief in his own ability had been lost. This was visible from seeing the posture that Agassi adopted when he walked on to the court. At the height of his playing career Agassi walked on to the court with almost a swagger. He had a purpose to his stride and this conveyed certainty to his opponent. - that he meant business. Contrast that with the physiology he adopted during his losing streak when he walked on to the court in a much more timid fashion – shoulders hunched and eyes down. This posture conveyed his own lack of self-belief and hence led to his poor performance on court.

The relationship between our physiology and our performance is summed up well in the diagram overleaf which has been modified from the Integrated Performance Model. What is relevant here is that our environment – not only the physical place we are in but also the people and objects contained therein – has an impact on our physiology and therefore our state of being. Just think about it. It is difficult to meditate in a busy supermarket as the environment is just not conducive to being still; there is too much activity happening. This is why when people meditate they typically go to a quiet place and sit down. Maybe they light candles. Their actions are designed to create an environment that is peaceful so their mind can slow down.

From my own experience I understand the importance of environment to my performance. For example, if my office and my desk are full of papers strewn all over the place, I know that I find it difficult to concentrate and my productivity subsequently decreases. There is something about the serenity and calmness of a tidy office that helps me keep my energy focused and concentrated and so I deliver better results. It is the same when I train horses. When I train my horses in a quiet place, particularly one they are familiar with, the training seems effortless. But put them in a noisy environment, especially one they are unfamiliar with, and their mind wanders. They simply can't focus on the task at hand because of all the distractions and so, frustration results for both parties.

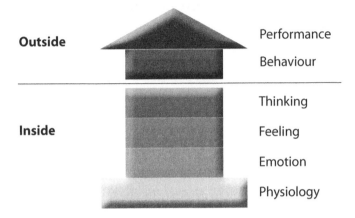

In Chinese literature much is written about the importance of environment and Roger Hamilton, founder of Wealth Dynamics, believes that certain types of environments are better for certain tasks. Within his office he has certain places where he goes to brainstorm on his business and other areas where he goes to undertake administrative tasks. Furthermore, there are places which he devotes to client meetings. I remember him once telling me about a business trip that he took and how he carved out certain spaces for particular tasks. The local café was where he brainstormed new ideas as the activity in the environment helped keep his mind active whereas the balcony on the roof of the hotel is where he made his telephone calls. I always found this fascinating because how often do we try to do all these different tasks in the same environment? There is an energy to environments just as there is to life and if we can harness the right environment for the right task, then the energy will flow and the task will be much easier to accomplish.

If it is not possible to change your environment, then one way to feel more energised is to move your body i.e. change your physiology. If you have been sitting for long periods of time then simply getting up and stretching your arms in the air can make a massive difference to how you feel. Last summer I was fortunate enough to attend the National Achievers Congress in London and Tony Robbins was the keynote speaker. He spoke for nearly four hours to over 7,000 people at the Excel Arena and managed to keep us all engaged and motivated throughout his entire presentation. So how did he do this? One way that he kept us all energised was by continuously changing our state. Tony would talk and then get us up out of our seats and get us to give the person next to us a shoulder massage. Then half an hour later he would get us to jump up and down. Tony understood that in order for the audience to stay interested in his material, they needed to stay engaged and one way to do this was to ensure that everyone's energy levels stayed high.

Many companies are beginning to realise the importance of environment to the productivity of their team members. This is why when I worked at Andersen, we had a few rooms designated as creative space areas where team members could brainstorm on new ideas away from the traditional workspaces. In her book, *I Wish I Worked There: A Look Inside the Most Creative Spaces in Business*, Kursty Groves examined twenty well known companies, including the LEGO Group, Oakley, Bloomberg and Urban Outfitters among others, and provided insights into how these firms use space in ways that promote creativity and collaboration, increase satisfaction and decrease employee turnover. In particular, she distinguished between *stimulating spaces* (that tell stories or enable people to access different information), *reflective spaces* (where people can go to focus or relax, as an individual or as a team), *collaborative spaces* (where people casually connect with one another, i.e. the cafeteria) and *playful spaces* (where people can bond through playing games, e.g. football).

Horses too are very sensitive to the energy of the environment that they are in with the result that their entire temperament can alter if they are in an energy state that does not resonate with them. Two of my friends have experienced this phenomenon when they have stabled their ex-racehorses on yards that are noisy and busy with activity. On both occasions their respective horses started to exhibit all kinds of stable vices like weaving (rocking back and forth), crib-biting, wind-sucking and box-walking. However, when the horses were moved to smaller, quieter yards these behaviours (which are typically deemed undesirable in the equine world) disappeared. So if the horses are so sensitive to the energy of the environment it stands to reason that they are super-sensitive to the different energies that people emit, and hence why they are 'energy barometers'. They read the energy and intent behind all our actions and can therefore challenge us when we are incongruent in what we are asking of them.

I'll never forget one Horse Assisted Coaching session I was running with a client called Monique. We were sitting in a paddock with a large grey horse called Marchador. I remember it was a warm sunny day and Monique and I were chatting about Marchador and how much she liked him. Then as we were sitting there, Marchador approached our chairs and began to enter our personal space. Having previously shown Monique how to ask Marchador to stay out of our space, I asked her to do this. So she got up slowly and using her body language she asked Marchador to leave by stepping towards him. Typically this action would result in the horse turning away and leaving but on this occasion Marchador kept approaching us. I asked Monique what was happening and it turned out that she really wanted Marchador to come up to her and nuzzle her face. Monique had no energy behind her actions and also no intent that Marchador should leave. Her actions as displayed by her body language were incongruent with her intent and Marchador could read that her energy was not serious and so continued his approach.

In fact, the interaction between Monique and Marchador reminded me of times when I was incongruent at work. Specifically, I remember a time that my boss wanted my team to undertake a project that I did not think was viable and believed was a waste of resources. On reflection it is therefore no surprise that the team members to whom I delegated the project failed to deliver. They could tell from my interaction with them that I was not serious about the project because I did not believe in it, and so my communication transmitted that energy. Contrast that with someone who is passionate about a project. When someone's entire being is passionate and committed to an outcome and they are focused and direct then that energy and enthusiasm transmits to others and they become engaged in the project. This is because emotional states are contagious and this is also why a positive environment can dissolve negative patterns of behaviour.

Be Present To NOW

'The most important rule in the horses'
code is to pay attention.'

Carolyn Resnick

Be Present To NOW

'The most important rule in the horses' code is to pay attention.'

Carolyn Resnick

As prey animals horses have to be continually alert to signs of impending danger. In other words, horses have to be very aware of the circumstances surrounding them – they have to be present to what is happening in order to ensure their safety. To maximise their chances of survival in the wild, horses have to have a wide field of vision which is why their eyes are located on the sides of their heads. The positioning of the eye means that the horse has a near 360 degree of vision, the only blind spots being directly between his eyes in the front and directly behind his tail. This is the reason that people are warned not to walk directly behind a horse because if you do you enter his blind spot, and if the horse is in any way anxious or concerned about his safety, he may kick out.

If you watch horses in the wild, predators nearly always attack from the back which is why the horse is very protective of this area of his body. Conversely, once a horse has implicit trust in you he will let you walk behind and even stand behind him with no concern whatsoever.

The great thing about being present and living in the moment is that horses are not concerned with what happened in the past or what is happening in the future. They have a mindset of now which is predominantly devoid of the fear that many humans have. In today's modern society it is rare to find people who live in the moment and who are present to their surroundings. In fact most people are so busy worrying about what is happening in their lives – whether that is concerns about the future or ruminating on events of the past – that they fail to notice what is happening around them. For many people this means that they fail to see the opportunities staring them directly in the face. If you are like me I'm sure you have all experienced a time when you lost something, say your keys. You look high and low and just cannot find them. All the time you are looking for the keys your mind is racing, thinking about the consequences of losing the keys: how will you start your car to pick up your children from school, how will you get into the house? The permutations are endless. Then eventually, when you resign yourself to the fact that you will never find the keys, they appear as if by magic right in front of you, in a place that you have already searched many times. It is almost as if you were blinded to seeing the keys while you searched for them.

In his book *Wink*, Roger Hamilton tells the story of a nine-year-old boy, Rich, who one day is entrusted by his sick father, a carpenter, to go to the Well of Wealth. His father had been depositing a dollar into the Well of Wealth for the last twenty years believing that if he gave generously to the well it would give back to him. Rich, however, does not follow the path to the Well of Wealth but another path and along the way meets an old woman, an optometrist, a plumber, a gardener, a fisherman, a rower, a musician, and an inn keeper. Each of these people shares a message with Rich concerning how they built their wealth. What is interesting is that it is not until he is at least halfway along his journey that Rich suddenly realises that along the way he has missed a myriad of opportunities to make money. As a carpenter's son he could have repaired benches for the gardener and sanded his window boxes. He could have helped the plumber, who had a property business, with carpentry jobs and for the rower he could have sanded and waxed his boats. The underpinning principle of the book is therefore *'What you see is always what you get.'* The challenge is that most of us do not see the opportunities around us as we are too wrapped up in our own worlds – we miss seeing the wood for the trees.

In my opinion, the lack of presence or mindfulness is becoming more of a problem as the fast-paced world we live in becomes more complex. Mobile communications mean that we are often available 24/7 resulting in no time to 'get away from it all and just be.' We spend more time living in the past or projecting ourselves into the future and so miss the joy and power of being in the present moment. Just think about how many training sessions you have attended physically but when your mind has been elsewhere, answering emails on your phone or just thinking about what else you should be doing at that time.

Mindfulness is a moment-to-moment awareness of your experience as it unfolds and unless you are present you miss what is happening around you.

On reflection I can now see how many opportunities have been presented to me in my life but I just did not see them at the time. In Chapter Five I described how my response to the suggestion that I went to work for Chuck Feeney in Spain meant that the job offer never resulted. At the time I never saw that as an opportunity but now I realise how my life could have changed if I had acted and responded differently to that situation; if I had been present to NOW. Now is a great acronym for:

N *No*

O *Opportunity*

W *Wasted*

Likewise, during my time working at Andersen and Deloitte, opportunities were regularly presented to me, which for some reason I failed to notice. One such opportunity arose in 2001/2 when I was approached by a competitor of mine to see if I could influence my then boss at Andersen to sell the business unit I was running to them. For me personally the deal would have been very lucrative as I would have become a shareholder in a larger business. At the time I was just a salaried employee but I often felt like a business owner because of the fact that I had created, nurtured and grown the business to become the global market leader in hotel performance metrics. Whilst I could see the personal gain that would come from selling the business I could not envisage my boss ever wanting to sell the business; at the time there was too much kudos involved in being part of this venture. Consequently I never seriously presented the opportunity to my boss. My lack of vision and clarity and inability to see what was happening around me made me blind to the upside. I was not present and mindful to what was happening. The net result was that some five years later, the competitor bought the business unit I had created and my job was made redundant. I was left with nothing but a redundancy cheque and good wishes. I often reflect and wonder how different my life would have been if I had recognised that opportunity for what is was and responded in a different manner.

The great advantage of being present and mindful, focusing on the here and now, means that we are better placed to listen and read situations accurately and to give appropriate responses. Consequently we can communicate and connect more effectively with others as we are able to respond in just the right way at just the right time. Horses can help us understand just how present and aware we are at any moment because if we are not present, then we don't know what is happening around us and so we cannot keep the horse safe from the next threat of attack. If the horse senses our lack of mindfulness he will be forced to step up into the leadership role and take charge of the situation. However, when we are mindful around a horse we are able to reach a deeper connection and receive a lot more information from him and the environment. Being a leader therefore means that you need to be present and aware at all times so that you can respond appropriately to the different situations that are presented to you.

Measuring Mindfulness

So how do you know if you are being present and mindful? Research from the Institute of HeartMath reveals that when we are present and mindful our heart rate variation is smooth and consistent and this is because there is a relationship between the brain and the heart. Many people believe incorrectly that the heart is constantly responding to 'orders' sent by the brain in the form of neural signals. However, the heart actually sends more signals to the brain than the brain sends to the heart! It is these impulses that cause us to have a 'gut reaction' or instinctive response. These heart signals have a significant effect on brain function, influencing emotional processing as well as higher cognitive faculties such as attention, perception, memory and problem-solving. In other words, not only does the heart respond to the brain, but the brain continuously responds to the heart.

HeartMath research has demonstrated that different patterns of heart activity (which accompany different emotional states) have distinct effects on cognitive and emotional function. During stress and negative emotions, when the heart rhythm pattern is erratic and disordered, the corresponding pattern of neural signals travelling from the heart to the brain inhibits higher cognitive functions. This limits our ability to think clearly, remember, learn, reason and make effective decisions. (This helps explain why we may often act impulsively and unwisely when we're under stress.) The heart's input to the brain during stressful or negative emotions also has a profound effect on the brain's emotional processes, actually serving to reinforce the emotional experience of stress.

In contrast, the more ordered and stable pattern of the heart's input to the brain during positive emotional states, like being present, has the opposite effect: it facilitates cognitive function and reinforces positive feelings and emotional stability. This means that learning to generate increased heart rhythm coherence, by sustaining positive emotions, not only benefits the entire body but also profoundly affects how we perceive, think, feel and perform.

> *"The Institute of HeartMath's research has shown that generating sustained positive emotions facilitates a body-wide shift to a specific, scientifically measurable state. This state is termed psychophysiological coherence because it is characterised by increased order and harmony in both our psychological (mental and emotional) and physiological (bodily) processes. Psychophysiological coherence is a state of optimal function. Research shows that when we activate this state our physiological systems function more efficiently, we experience greater emotional stability and we also have increased mental clarity and improved cognitive function. Simply stated, our body and brain work better, we feel better and we perform better."*

One great way to get into a state of mindfulness is to moderate your breathing, since breathing patterns modulate the heart's rhythm; it is possible to generate a coherent heart rhythm simply by breathing slowly and regularly at a ten-second rhythm (five seconds on the in-breath and five seconds on the out-breath). Breathing rhythmically in this fashion can thus be a useful intervention to initiate a shift out of a stressful emotional state and into increased coherence and thus mindfulness.

The Seasons of Business

If everything is composed of energy it follows that there is a natural ebb and flow to all activities, with times of contraction and times of expansion, which we can only be aware of by being present and mindful. You only have to look at the seasons to see this happening. Spring and summer are times of expansion whilst autumn and winter are times of contraction. People too have an ebb and flow to their lives and to be successful it is important that we recognise when our bodies need to rest and honour that time. In fact, most people resist the period of contraction and try taking more action which just leads to more contraction in their lives. During periods of contraction we feel weak, restricted, suppressed, frustrated, unhappy and tired. We don't feel like doing much and often this is a signal to the body that it needs to get clarity on what to do. Contrast this with periods of expansion when we want to take action as we feel energised, happy, joyous and have self-belief. If you were to compare these two time frames to a set of traffic lights, periods of contraction are the red 'Stop' light whilst periods of expansion represent the green 'Go' light. The challenge is that most businesses and people are so disconnected from what is happening around them (they are not present to NOW) that they fail to see these changes in seasons and so things become difficult as we are fighting against the natural flow of the environment.

Businesses also follow cycles which is why it is rare to find the same companies being the best performers year on year. Businesses, like people, need to recharge and refocus their efforts. They need a period of reflection. A great example of the fact that everything works in cycles can be seen in the DotCom crash of the late 1990s into the early 2000s. In 1998, graduates rushed to Silicon Valley to secure the myriad positions made available by fledgling internet companies. Billions of dollars were loaned to start-up companies and in 1999, most of the 457 IPOs were internet and technology related and 117 of these ventures doubled their share price on the first day of trading. Yet the rapid growth and expansion of the industry meant that it overstretched itself. Companies, whilst innovative, were not financially viable and so by late 2002 the entire market had crashed and imploded resulting in massive job losses. The industry needed to take time to reflect and re-focus on its priorities. As a result, the survivors of the DotCom crash such as Amazon are now thriving businesses in their own right - with owner Jeff Bezos now reportedly the 43rd richest man on the planet.

Latent Learning

Just as there is an ebb and flow to our lives and businesses there is also an ebb and flow to the learning cycle.

Neuroscience has shown that the conscious mind can only hold four 'chunks' of information for 30 seconds or less. This is why it is imperative that communication is clear and direct; any confusion and the message will get lost. When working and training horses I always recognise that I need to present one micro-subject at a time and keep it simple so that my horse can understand what I need him to do. Any time I try to make the lessons complex they invariably result in my horse failing to understand what is required. The other practice that it's important to recognise is that horses need time to process what we ask them. We often call this period of time latent learning. I cannot recount how many times I have allowed my horse some processing time; when he comes back to the task at hand he immediately gets what to do.

Back in 2006, during a sabbatical, I was working with a Quarter horse called Bunny at a horse rescue in Colorado. Bunny had not had a great start in life and had been very afraid of humans and particularly of being touched on his face and neck. Over a period of three months I worked with him to gain his trust so that he was happy to be touched all over, and following extensive groundwork he was ready to go off to another trainer to put him under saddle. In order for him to get to this trainer we needed to be able to load Bunny into a horse trailer. Since Bunny had only had limited exposure to being in a trailer I needed to train him to feel safe going into one. Over a period of weeks I gradually introduced him to the trailer and then I tried to encourage him to go into it. Initially Bunny was having none of it; he would approach the trailer and then rear, spin around and disappear to the far side of the pen.

I persisted in building his confidence and then one day he just walked in. No questions asked. He had just needed to process what was happening and once he understood he responded magnificently. There are so many cases I have seen where people have struggled to load a horse into a trailer and once they stop, let the horse rest and maybe go and get a cup of tea, when they come back the horse loads as if there has never been a problem.

Quantum Management

Presence is a rare quality in the frenetic twenty-second sound bite world we live in. Yet in the future it is believed that being present in the moment – alert, awake and neutral – will become a leadership imperative, as living in the past or endlessly worrying about the future is a waste of energy and resources. People with presence have an ineffable quality about them and are present simply by being attentive and undistracted. Horses encourage us to be present so that we can be attentive to their needs, and when I'm not they certainly let me know – typically by misbehaving to get my attention and bringing me back to the present moment. Personally, I recognise the challenge of staying present as it seems I continually focus on the things on my To Do list and what needs to happen next. The net result is that I miss opportunities that present themselves right in front of my eyes. Successful leaders in the future will need to combine that unique skill of being totally aware of what is happening around them with the foresight to see how this could convert to future opportunities. We are living in a time of unprecedented change, where all the old paradigms are being thrown away. Today, for companies to survive they need to adapt and this means that team members too must embrace this change. Everyone needs to assume responsibility for their own life and lead themselves in order to bring success to the entire business, because stress will result when team members feel powerless to embrace the changing environmental conditions.

CHAPTER ELEVEN

Dare To Be Different

*'The definition of insanity is doing the
same thing over and over again
and expecting different results.'*

Albert Einstein

Dare To Be Different

*'The definition of insanity is doing the same thing
over and over again and expecting different results.'*
Albert Einstein

Many times when I talk to my clients about the benefits of Horse Assisted Coaching they look at me and say, "Julia, are you mad, what can we learn about leadership, teamwork and communication from horses?" to which I reply, "Well, are you insane?" Albert Einstein once said, *"The definition of insanity is doing the same thing over and over again and expecting different results"* and yet I continue to witness individuals and companies investing thousands and thousands of pounds in coaching and training programmes that simply don't deliver as much value as they could.

My challenge to you today is, *"Are you prepared to be different and step outside the box and experience a whole new different type of training and coaching where the teachers are horses?"* Are you prepared to take yourself and your team members out of their comfort zone in order to achieve incredible results that will benefit both the company and the individuals? Unfortunately, often the answer to this question is 'No'. We are so conditioned to stay in the comfort of what we know that we don't want to be or do anything different. From a psychological point of view I understand this as we have an inherent need for safety but from a business and personal growth perspective, this leaves us stagnating and therefore we soon become bored and complacent. We delude ourselves that there are no other options because we have closed ourselves to the many opportunities around us.

At a recent Entrepreneurs Circle event I was exposed to the concept of 1-4-15-60-20, which helps explain why we don't dare to be different. The premise of this philosophy is:

- *1% of people are exceptionally rich and successful*
- *4% of people are prosperous*
- *15% of people are doing well*
- *60% of people are sustaining mediocrity and in financial terms are just keeping their head above water*
- *20% of people are poor and just shouldn't be doing what they are doing at all*

If we apply the 80:20 rule of business to this analogy it helps explain why 80% of businesses are mediocre. They don't stand out from the crowd and so attain only average results. So if you and your business want to be successful I challenge you to Dare to be Different and stand out from the crowd by engaging in some Horse Assisted Coaching to help you grow your business and people. As Mark Twain once said:

> *"Whenever you find you are on the side of the majority, it is time to pause and reflect. The majority in your business, industry or profession are wrong about most – if not all – of their beliefs about how to be successful in that business, industry or profession."*

So avoid the crowd and create a WOW factor in your business by looking at the development of your team and business from a different perspective.

Game Training – a new vehicle for a new era

We are all aware how the social media revolution is changing the way we do business but did you also realise that 'gamification' is becoming big news? For those of you that don't know, gamification is a way of engaging both clients and team members in initiatives through the use of games. People get awarded points for completing certain activities and this leads to prizes. Gartner Inc estimates that by 2014 more than 70% of the Global 2000 organisations will have at least one 'gamification' application and Matt Lent of The Game Trainers believes that by 2015 gameferencing (a conference run around a game theme) will be the rule and not the exception.

I personally first experienced gamification when John Assaraf launched the Praxis Now Community – a community of people committed to enhancing their own success through the use of neuroscience and brain retraining. During the launch phase you could get points for posting on the site, connecting with others, starting discussions etc. There were three gamification sessions with winners for each session and then overall winners. The top five gamers were flown to San Diego by John Assaraf for a day of masterminding at his home. It was an amazing prize that got all the community members engaged during the launch phase, so much so that many members opted to join the paid members community at the of the trial period. The experience was fun and rewarding and got everyone motivated to participate.

So what does gaming have to do with business and Horse Assisted Coaching?

Jane McGonigal suggests that a game consists of four elements, namely:

- *A goal, which gives participants a sense of purpose*
- *Barriers (better known as rules) which inspire strategic and creative solutions*
- *A feedback system, such as points or progress indicators, which provide motivation to keep playing*
- *Voluntary participation, so that players accept the three elements above*

These four elements fit nicely with the definition of business, as in simplistic terms:

- *Goal = business mission statement which might be to make money*
- *Barriers = could equate to the markets, competition, law and environment*

> ▓ *Feedback Process = key performance indicators*
> *e.g. profitability, market penetration*
> ▓ *Voluntary Participation = team members who have*
> *decided to work for the business*

So in essence we can conclude that business could be construed as a 'game' and if the right environment is created in which to hold the game then creativity and fun can occur as team members feel engaged, empowered, motivated and challenged. You only have to look at the ethos of some of the world's most successful companies of the last decade like Apple, Google, Yahoo and Facebook to realise that fun, creativity and innovation are at the heart of their business.

So how can Horse Assisted Coaching help your business?

Horse Assisted Coaching from my perspective is game training with horses. We create a fun, engaging experience where everyone is relaxed and, as a result, is fully engaged and receptive to learning new concepts. The latest research into the psychology of memory shows that intention to remember is a very minor factor in whether you remember something or not. Far more importantly, whether you want to remember something is how you think about the material when you encounter it. A classic experiment by Hyde and Jenkins in 1973 illustrated this perfectly. People were given a list of words which they were then later asked to recall. In remembering the words one group of people were asked to think about the word and how it made them feel, whilst the other group were asked simply to check if the word contained the letter e or g. The first group had to 'deep process' the material and link its relevance to themselves whilst the second group just had to 'shallow process' and indeed many of this group did not even read the word, they just sought to identify the two letters. The research concluded that the group which had 'deep processed' the information remembered twice as much as the group who had only thought shallowly about the words. Being immersed in a Horse Assisted Coaching session where there is a lot of reflection allows the client to really think about the material, and often we find that the best lessons from these sessions happen days or weeks after the event – this is when the AHA! moment occurs. Clients experience 'deep processing' which is why Horse Assisted Coaching works so effectively.

Can experiential activities help your individual contributors, teams and leaders develop collaboration and problem-solving skills?

I absolutely believe that participating in a Horse Assisted Coaching session will bring untold benefits to any organisation. In my experience, team members leave more focused and committed having had, in many cases, true insights into what is happening both in their personal and professional life. These AHA! (Accelerated Horse Awareness™) moments cause a quantum shift in people, allowing them to see things with a new perspective. Often a greater appreciation of the challenges faced by co-workers is observed, resulting in a more collaborative environment when team members return to work.

Trust is one of the major new commodities of the environment we live in and horses are great at helping individuals develop this essential life skill. Let's face it, if we don't trust the people we work with then we won't achieve much and all our energy will be taken up focusing on negative things and protecting our position. How much more effective can an organisation be when everyone trusts each other?

So how do employees learn these desirable character-istics? One way is to provide the employee with a mirror of their behaviour because they may not be aware of the traps they are falling into. They also need to know what they become under pressure. Traditional ways of creating this mirror are through coaching programmes or 360 degree feedback. The challenge with these practices is that they can lack objectivity because human intervention is required which could cloud the mirror.

Horses mirror the essential qualities of leadership – trust, authenticity, honesty, intuition, listening, a willingness of spirit and perseverance. They have no agenda with us. They simply reflect our strength of character, our heart, our internal incongruence and our self-limiting perceptions. Horses help us understand that leadership begins with who we are being. Horses help us close the gap between how we actually present ourselves to others and how we think we are being.

Horse Assisted Coaching provides a cost-effective means of getting that feedback as the horse mirrors exactly how you are feeling. Horses provide us with immediate, 100% non-judgmental, observable feedback, mirroring our internal reality. Living in the 93% of the non-verbal world of communication, they are not impressed by position, status or power. They cannot tell who is the CEO or who is the janitor. They just respond to what is presented to them.

So if you are looking for an innovative way to bring a different perspective to your leadership and team building trainings then please consider Horse Assisted Coaching. It's really effective, fun and the return on investment (ROI) is significant as personal breakthroughs can be achieved in minutes compared to months (or even years) of traditional coaching.

Horse Assisted Coaching might not yet be in the mainstream of learning and development but it should be, because in my experience most of the current offerings are not delivering on their promises and as Einstein stated, "We cannot solve our problems with the same thinking we used when we created them." So come on, try it and see what benefits you and your organisation can receive; I'm sure you will be pleasantly surprised because, as Plato noted, *"You can discover more about a person in an hour of play than a year of conversation."*

Hopefully by now I have managed to share with you why *"There is something about the outside of a horse that is good for the inside of a man"* and maybe one day you will allow the horse to become your teacher because there are so many skills that can be learned in the barn that translate back to the boardroom.

Unbridled Success Programmes and Retreats

Connecting to success and becoming a leader of your own life is always a team sport and horses are masterful teachers in this journey. So start taking action and move your life forward with some of the amazing resources I have to offer.

Unbridled Success Programmes and Retreats

The *Unbridled Success* Programmes and Retreats are for people just like you – people who are seeking to make a transformation in their lives and become more empowered through becoming better leaders. All the programmes and retreats form part of a safe, unique and truly memorable coaching experience. There is no riding as all the Horse Assisted Coaching sessions are carried out on the ground and it doesn't matter whether you have any horse experience or not. The opportunity for a breakthrough, whether in your business or personal life, is profound.

Whatever exercise you are engaging in with the horse, you are sure to get 100% unbiased instant feedback which is hard to ignore. The horses sense whether you are congruent and aligned in heart, body and spirit and so have an innate ability to see deep into your soul and challenge those beliefs and false self-images that our ego puts up to protect us.

Unbridled Success Programmes and Retreats focus on a number of key business and personal development areas including:

- *Leadership Begins with You*
- *Harnessing Authenticity*
- *Effective Communication*
- *Listening to Lead and Connecting to Success*
- *Developing Trust and Intuition*
- *Team Dynamics for Results*
- *Personal Influence and Power*
- *Maintaining Personal Boundaries*
- *Building Positive Relationships*

Coaching programmes are offered in Yorkshire, UK and across the world for:

- *Private 1:1 retreats*
- *Private groups*
- *Corporate retreats*
- *Team building*

Visit **www.businesshorsepower.com** for more information about creating a dramatic improvement in your business and life through increased focus, purpose and an ability to take action.

About the Author

JULIA FELTON is passionate about helping people transform so that they can be empowered to lead the life they desire. By unleashing their own powerful potential, individuals and teams can get into flow so that they can make more money and experience success without the stress. Her innovative coaching and development programmes for individuals, teams and organisations are committed to creating positive transformation and getting outstanding results through creating greater trust and flow.

By connecting to and acknowledging their unique natural strengths individuals, teams and organisations are able to become more motivated, productivity increases and organisational results improve. Collaboration reigns and competition is banished as teams work together with a singular purpose.

Julia's extensive corporate experience includes building businesses and teams from the ground up. During her 12 year career at Andersen and Deloitte she was responsible for developing a business from an idea on a piece of paper to creating and the building a million pound business unit that became firmly established as the global market leader in its niche. Her unique ability to work at both a strategic and tactical level means that she is sought after as a high performance consultant, mentor and coach.

Julia holds a degree in Hospitality Management and is a member of the Chartered Institute of Marketing and a Fellow of the British Association of Hospitality Accountants. She is also a qualified NLP practitioner and coach. She is also a Talent Dynamics Performance Consultant.

Julia's passion is horses and as a natural horsemanship coach and a Licensed HorseDream Partner she often incorporates sessions working with the horses into her *Unbridled Success* leadership and team working programmes.

Julia is an accomplished speaker and the author of *Unbridled Success* – How the Secret Lives of Horses can Impact your Leadership, Teamwork and Communication skills.

http://www.facebook.com/julia.m.felton

http://www.twitter.com/Julia_felton

http://uk.linkedin.com/in/juliafelton

References

Assaraf, John. *Having It All*. New York, Simon & Schuster, Inc. 2003

Camp, Joe. *The Soul of a Horse: Life Lessons from the Herd*. New York, Random House, Inc. 2008

Cashman, Kevin. *Leadership from the Inside Out*. San Francisco, Berrett-Koehler Publishers, Inc. 2008

Childre, Doc and Cryer, Bruce. *From Chaos to Coherence (the power to change performance)*. USA 2008

Covey, Stephen R. *The Speed of Trust – the one thing that changes everything*. New York, Simon & Schuster, Inc. 2006

Greene, Frank S. *Leadership Matters – The Leadership Guide*. 2006

Gunter, June Ed. D. *Teaching Horse – Rediscovering Leadership*. Bloomington, Author House, 2007

Hempfling, Klaus Ferdinand. *Dancing with Horses – the art of body language*. Vermont, Trafalgar Square Publishing, 2001

Hunting, Paul. *Why Talk to a Guru? When you can whisper to a horse*. Cambridge, Perfect Publishers Ltd., 2006

Ingram, Kathleen Barry. *Equine Facilitated Learning: Implicit Knowing versus Explicit Knowledge*. *http://sacredplaceofpossibility.com. 2008*

Kohanov, Linda. *Riding Between the Worlds*. Novato, New World Library, 2003

Kohanov, Linda. *Way of the Horse.* Novato,
New World Library, 2007

Landsberg, Max. *The Tools of Leadership.* London,
HarperCollins, 2001

Linacre and Cann. *An Introduction to 3-Dimensional Leadership.* 2001

Maxwell, John C. *Everyone Communicates Few Connect – what the most effective people do differently.*
Nashville, Thomas Nelson, 2010

Maxwell, John C. *The 21 Irrefutable Laws of Leadership – follow them and people will follow you.* Nashville, Thomas Nelson, 2007

Maxwell, John C. *Developing the Leader Within You.* Nashville, Thomas Nelson, 1993

Maxwell, John C. *The 17 Indisputable Laws of Teamwork.*
Nashville, Thomas Nelson, 2001

Kouzes, James M. and Posner, Barry Z. *The Leadership Challenge – Five Practices of Exemplary Leaders.* San Francisco, Josey-Bass, A Wiley Imprint, 2002

Resnick, Carolyn. *Naked Liberty.* California,
Amigo Publications, 2005

Roberts, Monty. *Horse Sense for People.* London,
HarperCollins, 2000

Strozzi, Ariana. *Horse Sense for the Leader Within.* Bloomington, Author House, 2004

Summerhawk, Kendall. *Brilliance Unbridled.* Heart of Success, 2006

Weber, Tracy Dr. *Synergy Medical Students Developing Emotional Intelligence Leadership Competencies through Equine Assisted Coaching.* August 23, 2005

Testimonials

*"In **Unbridled Success** Julia Felton has brought together the many strands of her expertise and knowledge and presented them in an insightful and engaging book. If you want to understand Horse Assisted Coaching and the benefits for you, your team or your organisation this is the book for you."*

David Harris – *Founder, Acorns 2 Oaks*

"Julia's ability to synthesize and organize complex emotional concepts in a clear concise manner makes this book powerful. It is perfect for business leaders who are looking to understand the key to successful teams and how to develop and nurture that success."

Sharolyn Wandzura - *Ears Forward Coaching*

"This is a powerful book and a must read for anyone seeking to make a sustainable change in their life"

Jackie Davis – *Stride 2 Success*

"Horse Assisted Coaching has had a profound effect on me as a leader. This innovative approach is at the cutting edge of 21st century human development. I believe everyone should experience this."

Steve Marsh – *Innovative Edge*

Lightning Source UK Ltd.
Milton Keynes UK
UKOW06f2243260815

257570UK00001B/4/P